Iraq:
Searching for Hope

Andrew White

continuum

First edition published in 2005 by

Continuum

The Tower Building
11 York Road
London SE1 7NX

80 Maiden Lane, Suite 704
New York
NY 10038

New edition published 2007
Reprinted 2008

www.continuumbooks.com

Copyright © Andrew White, 2005, 2007

All rights reserved. No part of this publication may be reproduced or transmitted in any form or by any means, electronic or mechanical, including photocopying, recording or any information storage or retrieval system, without prior permission from the publishers.

Scripture quotations taken from the HOLY BIBLE, NEW INTERNATIONAL VERSION. Copyright © 1973, 1978, 1984 by International Bible Society. Used by permission of Hodder & Stoughton Ltd, a member of the Hodder Headline Plc Group. All rights reserved.

Photographs 2, 4, 7 and 9 copyright © David Chancellor. Reproduced with permission. Other photographs courtesy of ICR/Coventry Cathedral.

British Library Cataloguing-in-Publication Data
A catalogue record for this book is available from the British Library.

ISBN 978–0–8264–9716–1

Typeset by Kenneth Burnley, Wirral, Cheshire
Printed and bound by MPG Books Ltd, Bodmin, Cornwall

Contents

Acknowledgements

This book is the story of my engagement with Iraq, and I have to thank first all those who have made it possible. Our staff in Baghdad, headed by Fadel Alfatlawi and including Samir and Nazera, are all simply wonderful. Without them, I would not have been able to do anything. I also want to thank the other eminent Iraqis who have enabled me to persevere in very difficult circumstances – there are so many but I will mention just three: Dr Mowaffak al-Rubaie, Georges Sada and Ambassador Sadoon al-Zubaydi. In the early days, Frank Wismer at the Coalition Provisional Authority in Baghdad gave me not just help but inspiration. I shall never forget his kindness and generosity.

Then there were so many outstanding diplomats, both British and American: Sir Jeremy Greenstock, Ambassador Paul Bremer, David Richmond, Dominic Asquith, General Mick Kicklighter, HE Edward Chaplin and, of course, the inestimable Christopher Segar. In London, we would not have been able to function without the team at the Foreign Office headed by Baroness (Liz) Symons, and not least the staff of the Global Conflict Prevention Pool. In Washington, I must acknowledge my friends at the Pentagon, especially Jerry Jones and Dave Patterson. I must also pay tribute to the US Institute of Peace, and especially Dr David Smock in Washington and Heather Coyne in Baghdad. Another exceptional ally has been Ward Scott at the American embassy in Baghdad, who has helped us in looking after the chapel, the church and the Centre.

In Coventry, I am deeply grateful to the whole team led by my colleague Justin Welby at the International Centre for Reconciliation. I must thank too all those who travelled with us on the long and difficult journey to Baghdad, including Tom Kingston, Oliver Scutt, Doug Roper, Jacob Florer, Court Clarkson, Daniel Kruger and R. T. Kendall. Of particular help with this book were Genevieve Galvin, Keren Lewis and Mark Powys-Smith – and I also have to thank the photographer David Chancellor for some of the pictures. My right-hand man for several years has been Jason Pennels, without whom I would not even have got to the airport. From the new Foundation for Relief and Reconciliation in the Middle East, I especially want to thank Christopher Segar (again), Richard Muir, Jayne Ozanne and those who have spiritual responsibility for me: Lord Carey, Bishop Colin Bennetts and Bishop Clive Handford.

In writing this book I am indebted to my editor, Huw Spanner, who has paid attention to detail in a way I find very difficult, and to my publisher, Carolyn Armitage, who first suggested that I write it. Once, she and I led a church home group together; today she is my commissioning editor.

I give thanks for the most wonderful wife and children: Caroline, Josiah and Jacob. Without them, I could not do what I do. They are the ones who really make the sacrifices every day as they cope with their fears for my safety. Then there are those who support us as a family, especially J. John and Killy, Mahesh and Bonnie Chavda and their church, and Bill and Connie Wilson.

Finally I give thanks to God and the angelic hosts for working overtime to protect me.

Historical note

Throughout this book, the recent war to liberate Iraq is referred to as the 'Third Gulf War'.

The First Gulf War was fought between Iraq and Iran between September 1980 and August 1988. It was occasioned by a dispute over the ownership of the Shatt al-Arab waterway, but the fundamental cause was Saddam Hussein's fear that the Islamist government in Tehran was encouraging Iraq's Shia majority to rise against him. Both sides resorted to chemical weapons and the massive bombardment of civilian populations. The war cost an estimated one million lives and left Iraq with debts of over $80 billion, owed principally to Kuwait.

The Second Gulf War (sometimes known simply as the 'Gulf War' or, in America, the 'Persian Gulf War') was fought between Iraq and an alliance of 28 countries led by America and including powerful contingents from Britain, France, Egypt and Syria. The occasion of the war was the annexation of Kuwait by Iraq in August 1990. A six-week air offensive by the allies began in January 1991 and was followed by a ground offensive lasting exactly 100 hours which stopped, controversially, at the borders of Iraq. An unknown number of Iraqi soldiers and civilians died – the new Iraqi Ministry of Defence estimates a total of 150,000 – while the allies lost no more than a few hundred. The legacy of the war included between two and three million refugees and very severe environmental damage after the retreating Iraqis blew up hundreds of oil wells and left them to burn.

Preface to second edition

Today, three-and-a-half years after the fall of Baghdad, I am still in Iraq. Things have deteriorated even further, but I still love it here. The search for hope has continued. At times, it has seemed to be futile, but we cannot stop looking. A few months ago, while I was sitting waiting for a helicopter in the fortified Green Zone, I realized that it was almost two decades ago to the day that I was asked at my interview for ordination what I would like to be doing in 20 years' time. I said I would like a parish in the London area, with some hospital chaplaincy work on the side. And here I am in Baghdad. I never dreamed I would be here in such circumstances, but I wouldn't want to be anywhere else. When I leave Iraq even for a short while, I am always longing to return.

The new final chapter of this book deals with my current work – how it has changed, how my Iraqi congregation has grown and what sustains us. The agony of this country goes on. Every day the news from Iraq on the radio and television is bad, but the reality is even worse. The scale of the tragedy is immense, and everything is in chaos. Nonetheless, we will not give up until Iraq is restored to its ancient glory.

Baghdad, 14 November 2006

Preface to first edition

As I sit in my room in Baghdad's International (or 'Green') Zone, I can hear the clatter of military helicopters and the rumble of tanks rolling by. Nearly two years after the invasion by Coalition forces, Iraq is a more dangerous place than ever. No longer can I wander the streets or drink tea in one of the city's many tea houses. Even my journey into the country is very different from days past, when we would drive from Jordan on the six-lane desert highway. Today we are brought in by the Royal Air Force from Kuwait and then flown the few miles to the Green Zone in an army helicopter with heavily armed and goggled soldiers leaning out of the sides covering the ground below.

The tragedy of this situation cannot be denied, yet the past few years of my engagement here have been a journey in search of hope. Once a cradle of civilization, Iraq has been the scene of immeasurable suffering in recent decades, both from the severe tyranny of Saddam Hussein and the Ba'th Party and from the extreme sanctions imposed by the UN after the Second Gulf War in 1991 – sanctions that were exploited and abused on every side. This book is the story of that search for hope, which took me from the palaces of the old regime through the streets of Baghdad to the makeshift offices of Coalition rule. It is a grim and often perilous journey. At times, I wondered if I would survive it. Yet for me it was a real challenge, diplomatic and spiritual, to work for the restoration of this nation and an end to its suffering.

Along the way, I attempt to answer some of the toughest questions this society poses, both political and theological, but I try to do it in an accessible way. This is not a book that pushes one particular political philosophy. Rather, it is meant to be an encounter with the whole of life as it is lived here, which deals with the most difficult issues, from the problem of kidnapping to the biggest question of all: 'Was the war justified?'

Despite all its current trials, Iraq has become a place I love more than almost any other. Some people long to ski in the Swiss Alps and some to shop on the Champs Elysées; I long to be in my beloved Baghdad. I invite you to come with me on this traumatic journey. You will meet the people who have inspired in me such a love for this country. You will see their suffering, their joy and finally their hope. For in the midst of the chaos there *is* hope, though at times it is very hard to find.

Baghdad, 7 March 2005

To my wife, Caroline,
and my sons, Josiah and Jacob,
and my dear friends,
David in Baghdad,
Jordan and Zoe
and Brett, Alyssa, Emily, Josiah, Nathanial,
Michaiah, Anna, Samuel, Jacob, Sophia, Destiny,
Judah, Sable, Megan, Rebecca and Nicholas
in Charlotte, North Carolina

Chapter 1

Making friends with the enemy

In 1998, the world was just beginning to wake up to the horror that was being inflicted on the Iraqi people as a result of sanctions. Nearly eight years had passed since the Second Gulf War at the start of 1991 and much was still unresolved. The West was deeply concerned by Iraq's failure to comply with UN resolutions, while the regime in Iraq was incensed by the misconduct of some of the weapons inspectors. I had just started my new job as director of international ministry at Coventry Cathedral, and with this role came the responsibility of directing the International Centre for Reconciliation (ICR).

The history of Coventry's role in reconciliation goes back to the night of 14 November 1940 – the night the Luftwaffe attacked the city. Hundreds of people were killed and many medieval buildings were destroyed – among them the great cathedral of St Michael's. The next morning, standing in the still-smouldering ruins, the Provost, Dick Howard, made a very brave statement. He pledged that, from that day on, Coventry would become a place of peace and reconciliation and that one day those who had done this would become our friends. Taking a piece of chalk, he wrote two words on the shattered wall of the sanctuary: 'Father, forgive.' (He didn't write 'Father, forgive them', he explained, because everyone needed to be forgiven.) Out of this resolve was to grow a worldwide network of places of reconciliation.

When I arrived in Coventry, the city's friendship with Germany (and in particular with Dresden) was long established. I was faced with a new challenge: which were the nations with whom we had to work towards reconciliation now? High on the list was obviously Iraq. No progress had been made in developing relations since the Second Gulf War. Two no-fly zones were in operation, one in the north and one in the south of the country, and the American and British planes that enforced them regularly came under fire from the ground. Meanwhile, the UN's weapons inspectors were being obstructed in their work and in response in December 1998 President Bill Clinton ordered major air strikes on Baghdad. There were now widespread reports of immense suffering in Iraq.

I made contact with the Iraqi-interest section of the Jordanian embassy (which was in effect the Iraqi embassy) and explained that I was from the ICR and wanted to see how we could help Iraq. But every time I requested a visa to visit the country, I was refused. The response was predictable: 'We don't want your help. Just stop the sanctions!' After weeks of frustration, I and my team were finally driven to prayer. As Archbishop William Temple once said: when you pray, coincidences happen and when you don't, they don't. Barely a day later I was introduced to a man who ran an organization promoting Anglo–Iraqi friendship and within hours I had received a personal invitation from Tariq Aziz, then Deputy Prime Minister of Iraq. A few days later, on 11 March 1999, I was on a plane to Amman in Jordan.

Early the next morning, I was met by the car that would take me the 660 miles to Baghdad. As we set off at dawn, I could hear the call to prayer from Amman's mosques and I was filled with both excitement and fear. Five hours of driving brought us finally to the border with Iraq. There was no mistaking which country we were entering: everywhere there were pictures of Saddam Hussein – Saddam hunting, Saddam at prayer, Saddam with a child on his knee, Saddam dressed like an English gentleman. I had never before been in a place so dominated by its head of state. There was nothing else to look at in the extraordinarily shabby VIP lounge. In the duty-free shopping section a cabinet displayed, at exorbitant prices, a frying pan and an electric kettle.

Two hours later I was allowed to continue on my journey. Once we had crossed the border the road was much better, totally straight and seemingly endless, and within minutes we were travelling through the featureless desert at 110 m.p.h. Even at that speed, it was several hours before we came to the first town, Ramadi. Next, across the river Euphrates, we reached Falluja. I had never heard of this city before and would never have guessed how infamous it was soon to become.

My arrival in Baghdad was unremarkable. The only thing that really struck me was the fact that almost every car I saw had either a broken windscreen or none at all – the result of sanctions, my driver explained. I was taken to al-Rashid, the government-owned hotel that was supposed to be the best in the country. A mosaic on the floor in the entrance portrayed not Saddam Hussein for once but George Bush Senior, with the caption underneath, in Arabic and English, 'Bush is Criminal'. Here I was met by people from the protocol department of the ministry of foreign affairs. It didn't take me long to work out that in fact they belonged to Saddam's intelligence service, the Mukhabarat. They were to be my minders, protectors and enforced friends. One of them, a quiet man called Jaber, was actually good company and in time I became rather fond of him.

The hotel had the feel of a Stalinist institution. My room was spartan, the sheets on the bed were grey with age and the water in the taps contained so many chemicals it burned your face. On every landing sat a man who did nothing but note down when you entered your room and when you left it. The television barely worked and showed only programmes portraying Saddam as some romantic, godlike Arab icon. It was not until the following day that I was taken to meet anyone. Then, accompanied always by my minders, I visited a range of religious and political leaders, including both Sunni and Shia clerics and Christian bishops. They all spoke on a single theme: the devastating effect of sanctions.

I was taken to the children's hospital and shown a pitiful succession of patients, many so ill that they didn't even cry. All of them, I was told, were dying as a result either of the sanctions or of the effects of depleted uranium – another constant theme. I was then taken to see the Minister of Health, Dr Umid Mubarak. Although he wore the same green uniform as the rest of Saddam's cabinet, he seemed very different from the other members I had met. He was a gentle, sincere and sophisticated man, Kurdish in origin. Not only did he care passionately about the people of Iraq, but I had the sense that he too was somehow a victim. I was to have many more meetings with him, and in time we became friends. After the war I would learn from him something of what really went on under Saddam.

The highlight of the week was meant to be the meeting with Mr Aziz. We had a long and very cordial conversation, from which it emerged that he was pleased to see me and wanted me to come back soon with some bishops and other church leaders. The most important things I came away with were an open invitation to return as often as I liked and permission to restore and use the Anglican church of St George of Mesopotamia in Baghdad.

I had already visited the church and was rather shocked by the state it was in. A caretaker had recently been appointed, but no one had ever explained his duties to him and as a result the building was filthy and infested with pigeons. He was a man named Hanna who still bore the scars of 17 years of internment as a prisoner of war in Iran, where he had suffered all the more for refusing to renounce his Christian faith. Within days the church was clean and tidy, a respectful place of worship – even if it looked more like a Chaldean Catholic church, with lots of plastic flowers, pictures of Mary and burning incense.

It wasn't long before I had arranged to return to Iraq, this time accompanied by various senior churchmen including the Bishop of Coventry (Colin Bennetts), the Bishop of Kingston (Peter Price) and the Bishop of Cyprus and the Gulf (Clive Handford) – who had, in fact, himself been the rector of St George's for a short while in 1967. This second visit was also constructive. As well as all the key people I had met before, we saw the then UN humanitarian co-ordinator in Iraq, Count Hans von Sponeck, a highly impressive man who told us of his grave concern about the way the sanctions regime was being administered, which was adding unnecessarily to the suffering of the Iraqi people. He assured us that it was a Western lie that Saddam's regime was stockpiling medicine and food and so creating the shortages itself – which, after the war, we discovered was in fact partly true.

Another very impressive person we met was Margaret Hassan, the director in Iraq of the humanitarian organization Care International, who I was to meet many more times in the years ahead. She was married to an Iraqi and was totally committed to the cause of the Iraqi people. She too told us of her many concerns for the ordinary people who were being made to suffer both by their government and by the sanctions the UN had imposed. Five years later, my team would be involved in the search for this wonderful woman after she was taken hostage.

By far the most significant meeting on this visit was with Georges Sada, the president of the Protestant Churches of Iraq. He was a cultured and very intelligent man who had risen to the rank of air vice-marshal in the Iraqi airforce before he retired in 1986. He was also a passionate Christian. Within days he would become my right-hand man and after a couple of years, when we knew we could really trust each other, he would tell me what was really going on in his country – often during long walks in the night to escape my minders. He was to prove indispensable as our work in Iraq developed, and as I look back I can't help feeling that that first encounter with him was a divine appointment.

I soon discovered that one item on everyone's agenda was a visit to al-Amiriya, the air-raid shelter bombed by the Americans in February 1991 that had become a memorial to the hundreds of people – mostly women and children – who had died there. It was used by the Iraqis for propaganda purposes, but there was no doubt that it was a very bleak place that still stank of death and spoke clearly of the horror of war. The woman who showed me around had lost nine of her own children there and had only survived herself because she had left the shelter for a few minutes to get them some food. A laser-guided bomb had hit while she was gone, cutting through ten feet of reinforced concrete to turn the shelter into a pressure cooker as its heating system exploded. There was flesh still stuck to the walls, but by far the worst thing I saw was the images of women and children blasted into them. One image, of a mother holding an infant, resembled a picture of a Madonna and child. Over the years, I have visited this shelter many times and it has always been an awful experience, but it is that image in particular that will never leave me.

Finally, with almost no notice, we were taken to see Mr Aziz. A fleet of presidential cars whisked us from the hotel, speeding down the middle of main roads and jumping traffic lights all the way to the rather tatty office of the Deputy Prime Minister. The meeting was formal but very friendly. Mr Aziz thanked me for coming back so quickly and then ran through the now familiar litany: the evil nature of the sanctions, the wickedness of the West and the need for our help. He ended with a request. Now that important religious leaders from Britain had visited his country, he wanted us to arrange for religious leaders from Iraq to visit not only Britain but also America. It would be a major undertaking, but we agreed to try.

I set about trying to organize this on my return to Coventry. By far the harder part was the American leg, but at Mr Aziz's suggestion I asked Billy Graham and his team for assistance and they proved to be invaluable. In due course we were told the names of the three Iraqis who were to come, and I was pleased to see that I had already met two of them: Ayatollah Hussein al-Sadr, who would represent the Shia, and the Chaldean Catholic patriarch, Raphael I Bidawid. New to me was Sheikh Dr Abdel Latif Humayem, a senior Sunni leader and a close confidant of Saddam.

It was in September that I flew to New York to await them for the first leg of their trip. Dr John Akers, Dr Graham's special assistant, who had spent many hours arranging the trip, was waiting for me at the airport. We were expecting the Iraqis later that night, but then word arrived that they were still detained in Amman, where the American embassy was subjecting them to a considerable inquisition before it would give them visas.

The following morning, I went to see Dr Graham in his room at the Marriott Marquis New York on Times Square. I spent over three hours with him and found him to be one of the most amazing people I have ever met. Never before had I encountered somebody so inspiring and yet so humble. As he became increasingly frail, his staff kept urging him to do only those things that nobody else could do – and dealing with Iraq was one such issue. We discussed the plight of the Iraqi people in great depth before turning our attention to the problems we were encountering in getting our three guests into America. The CIA had presented us with a report on each of them. They were not very accurate, but there were two things that caught our eye. The first was that a relative of the ayatollah had recently been killed by Saddam – in fact, a very close relation, the father of the now notorious radical

Muqtada al-Sadr. The second was that the CIA described the sheikh, who was the principal preacher on Iraqi television every Friday, as the 'Billy Graham of Baghdad'.

The news from Amman was still not good. We discussed every possible way Dr Graham might use his influence to secure the visas, and one of his aides even suggested contacting the White House. Dr Graham was silent for a moment and then said that Mr Clinton was 'morally compromised at the moment'. This was just after the President's affair with Monica Lewinsky had become public knowledge. Dr Graham was clearly aware of his huge moral authority in the world and didn't want to abuse it in any way.

It was five days before the Iraqi delegation was allowed into America, and when they did finally arrive they were treated with great suspicion: photographed, fingerprinted and further inter-rogated. They had missed most of the many meetings we had scheduled – I had had to speak on their behalf – but they did have a very fruitful time with Dr Graham, who showed a real concern for the suffering of their people. Subsequently, they were treated to a flight over the Niagara Falls in a private plane before meeting the former President, Jimmy Carter.

I was determined that they should have a much better experi-ence coming to Britain, and when they arrived three days later they were given a VIP welcome. Their hectic itinerary, which was well covered by the media, started in Coventry and ended in London, where we met with various political and religious leaders, including George Carey, then Archbishop of Canterbury. We were assisted throughout by two Iraqi friends living in Britain: Fadel Alfatlawi, a postgraduate student in computing who several years later would be running the Iraqi Institute of Peace in Baghdad, and Wafir al-Ghabban, an environmental engineer I had just happened to meet one day on the London-to-Coventry train.

It quickly became obvious that the ayatollah had to be very careful what he said and who he met, particularly if they were Muslims – and it was some time before I got my first opportunity for a brief conversation with him that wasn't watched by other, rather shady Iraqis. He had complained of pains in his legs and had asked if I could take him to a doctor. For a few moments in the waiting room I had the chance to talk to him frankly about the difficulties he was facing, though it was only later that I learned that his entire family was under house arrest while he was out of the country. It was not until after the war that we were able to talk freely again, and he told me only then that the chronic pain in his legs was the result of torture at the hands of Saddam's regime.

One of the most significant meetings took place at the Royal Institute of International Affairs at Chatham House. The lecture hall was packed. Several of the more dubious Iraqis were there and so I knew the ayatollah would not say much. In fact, the man who talked most was the patriarch, who spoke eloquently of the plight of his people and their desperate desire to be relieved from their suffering and isolation. After the speeches there was a time for questions. Suddenly, a group of people from the Shia al-Khoi Foundation stood up and, unrolling a large banner with over two hundred faces pictured on it, asked the ayatollah to tell the audience who these people were.

There was a moment of poignant silence, and then in reply the ayatollah recited some words from the Qur'an. Again he was asked the same thing and again he responded with some words from the Qur'an. In the end, the questioner gave the answer himself: everyone pictured on the banner was a member of the ayatollah's own family who either had been killed or had disappeared. This was the sad reality of the fate of Iraq's Shia community.

At the back of the audience stood a friend of the ayatollah, a doctor by the name of Mow Baker. They had not seen each other for over 30 years, since Dr Baker had fled to London and the ayatollah had accompanied him to the airport. This evening, they did not speak to each other – it was far too dangerous – but the tears rolled down their cheeks as they looked at each other across the hall. They were not to meet again until after the war, when Dr Baker returned to his motherland and resumed his old name, Mowaffak al-Rubaie. He would then quickly be appointed to the Iraqi Governing Council and would later be given a five-year contract as National Security Adviser by the American administrator and 'ambassador', Paul Bremer. Within weeks of the end of the war he would be one of my closest colleagues, and eventually he was to become the chair of the Iraqi Institute of Peace.

This visit formed some lasting and strategic relationships, many of which we would only take full advantage of after the fall of Saddam. It also sealed our relationship with the Christian, Sunni and Shia communities of Iraq. The three men may have arrived in Britain as an official delegation but they departed as friends. In Coventry, we had presented them with a copy of the famous Cross of Nails made from three nails that fell from the roof of the medieval cathedral as it burned on that night in 1940. It is recognized as a symbol of the death of our Lord but also, more specifically, of peace and reconciliation between nations. The cross we presented was set in a stone from the ruins of the old cathedral, and on it a plaque said simply: 'To the people of Iraq – Father, forgive.'

On a subsequent visit to Iraq, I asked the patriarch what had become of this cross. He took me to his car and there it was, on the back seat. He explained that it said, 'To the people of Iraq' and so wherever he went to say Mass he would place it on the altar to remind the people that they were not forgotten. After the war, when the situation in Iraq was really bad, the cross was again taken out by his successor, Immanuel Deli, and was seen by many on TV.

From now on I went to Iraq several times each year, meeting all the usual people and getting to know many of them very well. Tariq Aziz in particular insisted that I always go to see him and he would greet me with great warmth. To some extent, I realized, I was being used by the regime, and I became a familiar face on Iraqi television condemning the sanctions. This was to prove a mixed blessing after the war, as some people saw me as a friend of the Iraqi people and others as a dupe of the old regime. The latter view was certainly taken at the time by the desk officers at the British Foreign Office, and they told me so in no uncertain terms. On one occasion, my Mukhabarat minder, Jaber, informed me that I had been invited to dine with Saddam's two sons. I said that I wouldn't go – but the look of terror on his face told me what that answer would mean for him, and so I did. It left an unpleasant taste when Uday and Qusay thanked me for all I was doing to help their country.

Our work was a mixture of trying to open channels of communication and trying to relieve people's suffering. One of the major humanitarian exercises we were involved in was helping to set up Iraq's first-ever bone marrow transplant centre, at the Saddam Medical City in Baghdad. The Minister of Health, Dr Umid Mubarak, had put us in contact with the man who was overseeing this, Dr Abdel Majid Hammadi, an outstanding clinician who had made some big advances in his field of haematology. He had invented a technique whose patent was sold for several million dollars – for which he was rewarded with $1,000 and a watch with Saddam's face on it.

The minister asked me if there was any way I could arrange for training for the medical team at what was to be called, inevitably, the Saddam Bone Marrow Transplant Centre. After many months of negotiation and planning – and thanks to the generosity of Sir Richard Branson and the charity Medical Aid to Iraqi Children – they finally arrived in Britain to study for several weeks under Dr Tony Darbyshire at the Princess Diana Children's Hospital in Birmingham. I remember vividly their final night in England, when we went out for dinner. None of them wanted to go back to Iraq, and the nurse on the team sobbed as she said, 'There is such freedom here!'

My trips to Iraq continued in much the same vein until 11 September 2001. I was in my office at Coventry Cathedral preparing to leave for Baghdad when the terrible news broke of the attacks on the World Trade Center and the Pentagon. As the enormity of the atrocity became apparent, it was clear that my relationship with Iraq was never going to be the same again. When I arrived in Baghdad a few days later, I found the city evidently as much in shock as the rest of the world. The Ba'thist leadership had fled as soon as they heard the news, fearing imminent 'reprisal'. Saddam was the only national leader not to condemn the attack at once, though he appeared to do so a few days later.

I had my usual meeting with Tariq Aziz and as I walked into his office he exclaimed, '*Abuna* [which means 'Father'] Andrew, tell them we had nothing to do with it! We are revolutionaries, not terrorists.' I responded without thinking: 'Your Excellency, it doesn't matter whether you are terrorists or revolutionaries, they are still coming to get you.' We sat and talked about the attack and the impact it would have on his country. The Iraqis were beginning to realize that, whether or not they had been involved, their time of reckoning was coming – and it was coming soon.

As I left Iraq, there was the first talk of a 'war on terror'. It was already known that al-Qa'ida was probably responsible for '9/11', but the Iraqis knew that as the most hated nation in the world they would have to pay part of the price. It wasn't long before the threats against them began. The war in Afghanistan was now under way, and everyone was talking about 'weapons of mass destruction' (WMDs). I had to admit I had heard countless stories about such weapons from my friends in Iraq, including tales of loved ones who had died while helping to transport them. It seemed obvious that WMDs existed and were being moved around. The big debate concerned the UN weapons inspectors – who should go and what they should do.

The British and American governments were suddenly very interested in our work in Iraq. Having long been regarded as a maverick who strayed into forbidden territory, I was now seen as a source of potentially important information. They were also interested in Georges Sada and encouraged us to bring him to London. Meanwhile, the storm clouds were gathering. Hans Blix, the chief UN weapons inspector, was under huge pressure to get into Iraq and find WMDs quickly. Around the world there was a growing number of demonstrations against the threat of war. It was in this atmosphere that I was asked by the Iraqi government to return to Baghdad and, knowing how urgent the situation was though not whether I could hope to achieve anything, I decided to go.

I went in October 2002. I knew it would be my last visit before the war, but I was not prepared for what I encountered. By now I knew many Iraqis and had many good friends among them, and they had always pleaded with me to do whatever I could to bring an end to the sanctions that had caused so much suffering. This time, however, the mood had changed. They knew war was coming because they were following the news closely.

I can remember the day the British government published the first of its two 'dossiers' on Iraq – the one that was later to be dismissed as 'sexed-up'. Access to the Internet had just been laid on for foreigners in al-Rashid and scores of journalists gathered around the monitors to see what the document contained. I too examined it, but with Iraqis and in particular former soldiers, who went through it with me carefully and told me what was accurate and what was not. On another occasion, I sat in a military officers' club one lunchtime and listened as senior people spoke openly of the biological and chemical weapons programmes. They told me it would be almost impossible for the inspectors to find them.

But what really impressed me were the comments of ordinary people on the street. I was the only Westerner that many of them had ever met, and when they addressed me they were addressing the West. One person after another told me of their desire that the regime should fall. A common refrain was: 'This time, don't let them stop until they have finished the job.' Never before had I heard people speaking in this way against the tyrant who watched them from every corner. They knew the risks they were running, but they had suffered enough and they believed that a war to overthrow Saddam was their only hope of freedom. Everyone knew that it was going to be a disaster – but what they were living through could no longer be borne.

From the usual round of politicians I heard nothing but defiance. Tariq Aziz was adamant that if necessary the Iraqis would fight – and fight hard. He told me that in fact the 'war on terrorism' had been launched by Iraq and informed me at length that the real terrorists were the Americans. Finally, he asked me if I would lead a team that would monitor the weapons inspectors and appealed to me to get other religious leaders involved. He offered me a car, an office, everything I would need to do the job. It did not take me long to decide that this was not a good idea. The voices on the street had convinced me that Iraq simply had to be liberated.

On my last night in Baghdad, I went for a walk with an Iraqi Christian. It was a wonderful warm evening, the stars were shining and there was a bright full moon. I asked my friend, 'How can you keep going when everything seems so dreadful?' Without hesitation, he replied with some words from the prophet Habakkuk (3.17–18):

> Though the fig-tree does not bud
>   and there are no grapes on the vines,
> though the olive crop fails
>   and the fields produce no food,
> though there are no sheep in the pen
>   and no cattle in the stalls,
> yet I will rejoice in the LORD,
>   I will be joyful in God my Saviour.

As we walked back to my hotel, the gigantic crossed swords of Saddam's Victory Arch seemed to reach the sky. Here, heaven and hell met. As I flew back to Britain the next day, I felt intense fear for the people of Iraq. I just hoped that a horrible ending would be better than unending horror. I hoped in vain.

Chapter 2

The struggle begins

From the start of 2003, the momentum towards war seemed unstoppable. The debate over WMDs continued, with daily reports from the weapons inspectors bringing mixed messages from Iraq, but already huge military forces were massing in the Gulf. When on 15 February anti-war demonstrations brought millions of people out onto the streets of the world's major cities, their protests already seemed futile.

America and Britain were seen increasingly as 'going it alone'. On 5 March, France, Germany and Russia issued a joint statement declaring that they would 'not let a proposed resolution pass [in the Security Council] that would authorize the use of force' against Iraq. The resolution in question, tabled by Britain, America and Spain, was finally withdrawn 12 days later after the French had threatened to veto it. The Leader of the House of Commons, Robin Cook – a former Foreign Secretary – resigned from the British government in protest at its willingness to go to war without the specific sanction of a UN resolution. The following day, President George Bush gave Saddam an ultimatum to leave Iraq within 48 hours or face invasion.

Shortly after this deadline expired, on 20 March 2003 at 02.30 GMT, the first strikes on Baghdad by cruise missiles and stealth fighters began. None of us had wanted this. War is always dreadful and yet it now seemed the only solution to an escalating crisis. My response to the prospect of battle was now very different from my feelings in 1991, for now I knew many people in Iraq. Indeed, I loved many people in Iraq. The days that followed were very painful for me emotionally, even though I was convinced that there was no alternative. At first we were still able to make contact with friends in Baghdad, who spoke of a mixture of fear and hope. No one could sleep for the pounding of the city through the night.

The military campaign progressed far more quickly than most of us had imagined, and there was much less retaliation than we had expected. By day two, most of Basra had been captured with little resistance and Baghdad was being heavily bombarded. The bombing appeared to be well targeted, but by day three stories were beginning to come through of civilian casualties. On 23 March, there were reports of over 100 civilians dead and many injured. One of the most distressing images was of the little boy Ali Ismail Abbas lying in hospital, having lost his whole family and lost both his arms.

There was intense debate over the justification for the invasion. The rapid advance of the troops did not seem to be weakening the opposition to the war. For much of its duration I was in Jerusalem, just as I had been in the Second Gulf War. Everyone there had been issued with gas masks and many had created sealed rooms in their homes for fear of a chemical attack on Israel. In 1991, many Scud missiles had landed in Tel Aviv, though fortunately no one was killed. There was no repeat of that this time, but the fear of it was very real.

From Jerusalem I would regularly phone my friends in Baghdad until the telephone exchange was hit and all direct contact ended. The last report we heard was from Dr Majid. He told us that one of his first successful bone-marrow-transplant patients had been too scared to stay in Baghdad while it was under constant attack and had discharged herself from hospital. Out of a sterile environment, with her immune system suppressed, her future was bleak. Eventually we heard that she caught an infection and died.

Georges Sada was now in London with his son. Saddam had allowed him to come with me, after my last visit to Baghdad, to present his greetings to the new Archbishop of Canterbury, Rowan Williams, who had been outspoken in his opposition to the war. Georges was regularly consulted by the British government and was always forthcoming, though he was careful to make clear that his military knowledge was 12 years out of date. I didn't attend any of these meetings, but I received a full account of one occasion when he spent most of the time telling the officials about Jesus. This must have been somewhat unexpected from an Iraqi former air vice-marshal.

As the war progressed, I spent much of my time talking with various people about the reconstruction that must follow it. During this period I made several visits to Washington for discussions with different government agencies. Their lack of knowledge about Iraq was very obvious and at times quite disturbing. It was clear that most of their information had been acquired by the intelligence agencies from the Iraqi opposition, and much of it was obsolete. I was in a difficult position. I was first and foremost a priest working for reconciliation and I did not want to become a source of intelligence, yet it was important that the American authorities should know what they were dealing with. In reality, I'm not sure that they did.

It wasn't easy to think about the future of Iraq when it was still being battered daily from the sky. Communication with Baghdad was by now impossible and we depended on what was reported or shown by the media. The stories that were coming out were horrible. I felt totally powerless. I didn't know what was happening to my many friends – it was impossible to make contact with anyone. The pronouncements from the Iraqi Ministry of Information and from the Coalition were totally at odds. The minister, Mohammed Said al-Sahhaf, whom I knew a little and liked, had earned the sobriquet 'Comical Ali', and at times it was indeed funny to hear him; but at other times it was very sad. The ministry was right next door to St George's and I was worried about the damage that might be done to our church, and to the caretaker and his family, when it was inevitably attacked.

Particularly disturbing were the deaths of several journalists. There were almost daily accounts of people being killed while seeking only to show the outside world what was happening. Meanwhile, much of the international community continued to condemn the war until its very end and beyond it. It was now obvious that Saddam was the real issue and some said that there had been too little effort to bring him down by other means.

By the end of March, the war was clearly coming to a conclusion. Coalition forces were nearing the capital and the Iraqi Minister of Information was looking increasingly absurd. On 9 April, he made his last and perhaps most famous statement – 'I triple guarantee you, there are no American soldiers in Baghdad' – even as an Abrams tank could be seen over his shoulder entering the city. The fighting was all but over – or so everybody hoped. Hours later, the most vivid pictures of the war were caught in the main square of Baghdad, right next to the Palestine and Sheraton Hotels, when a large statue of Saddam was pulled down by American troops with the help of locals. It was the perfect image of the dictator's fall. As the statue toppled, there were scenes of great jubilation. The evil regime of Saddam was now gone, gone for ever. People took off their shoes and beat his image with them – in Arabic societies, a sign of the deepest contempt.

But hope very soon turned to horror. The very next day, I was deeply shocked when I saw a news flash that Ayatollah Abdel Majid al-Khoi had been assassinated at a mosque in the holy city of Najaf. He was the uncle of Yosef al-Khoi, a leading member of the Iraqi opposition whose al-Khoi Foundation had displayed their banner at Chatham House in 1999, and I had known them both for several years. Only a few days before, the ayatollah had come to speak with me at a conference at Windsor Castle where I had just delivered a paper on religion and violence to a select gathering of Christians, Jews and Muslims. As we sat and talked, he told me he had been asked by the Americans to return to southern Iraq as soon as possible to help with the task of reconstruction, and he asked if I would be prepared to go with him. I said that I thought it was still too early to make such decisions. Now he was dead.

Ayatollah al-Khoi was a good man, still young, who had so much to offer. His murder was essentially a result of the tension between different Islamic clans, all Shia but all competing for power and control. It was an ominous warning of the trouble that could be expected to break out as soon as Iraq had been finally released from its oppression.

For some time now we had been contacting the Foreign Office to point out the serious problems that could erupt and to suggest some initiatives that could help to prevent them. Iraq has one of the most complex societies in the world. Besides the Kurds and the Assyrians, there are several hundred Arab tribes, ranging in size from a few thousands (such as the Chalabi clan) to well over half a million (such as the Fatlawis). Some of these are concentrated in one place, while others are dispersed throughout the country – but even the most cultured and cosmopolitan Iraqis have a strong sense of ethnic and tribal allegiance. Overlaid onto this are religious divisions. The large Sunni Muslim minority despise the Shia majority as heretics.

Our biggest concern was that there would be conflict between the Sunna, who had generally supported Saddam and had been rewarded for it, and the Shia, who he had so long persecuted and oppressed. We were also anxious about the fate of Iraq's 700,000 Christians. They had enjoyed a degree of favour from the old regime and might now suffer for it – and they might also bear the brunt of any resentment over the invasion of Iraq by the 'Crusaders' of the West.

Moreover, apart from the tensions between the different *houzat* (the Shia seats of religious learning) that had been bottled up under Ba'thist rule, there was also uncertainty over the influence the more radical Shia of Iran might exert over their co-religionists across the border. Several prominent Iraqi Shia had been living in exile in Iran for many years and no doubt they would now want to return. The situation was going to be very volatile, and the prospects for religious harmony in the new Iraq did not look good.

The response from the Foreign Office, however, had been polite but firm. The immediate priority was to sort out the basics such as water and electricity. Dealing with these other issues came a long way down the list.

On 1 May, President Bush landed on the home-coming aircraft carrier USS *Abraham Lincoln*, 30 miles off the coast of California, and declared that major combat operations in Iraq had ended. It was a remark he would come to regret.

Why me?

My great friend and mentor Lord Coggan used to say, 'Don't take care. Take risks.'

Unlike most people working in Iraq today, I am there not because I have to be but because I want to. A willingness to take risks is one of the fundamental values of the International Centre for Reconciliation, because it is fruitless to work for peace if you are not prepared to risk anything. The very nature of conflict, and therefore of conflict resolution and reconciliation, is that it takes place in some hostile environments.

I often ask myself, 'Why me?' It isn't an easy question to answer, but one thing I am sure of is that I feel an immense love for all the peoples of the Middle East. I have worked closely for many years with Iraq's different religious, tribal and ethnic groups, and I thank God that I was able to form many solid relationships before the start of the recent war. They have provided the foundation for what I am trying to do now. It also helps that I have had the opportunity to study the various religions that hold sway in this region, while being absolutely secure in my own Christian faith. But I have not been involved in any attempts to try to reconcile, or syncretize, different religious beliefs (which is often seen in the Middle East as showing disrespect for them).

This is not a task one undertakes lightly, for it involves many sacrifices. By far the greatest is that it is impossible to live the conventional life of a husband and father when one is involved in such radical and dangerous work. I often long to be with my family while I'm away. Occasionally they have been able to join me on overseas trips, but Iraq is no place for a holiday. I can't pretend that being away from those I love most is easy. I try to ensure that when I am home they are my top priority, but even that is hard, as so many people want to see me when I am in

England, not least my staff. I am very fortunate to have a wife and children who support me totally in my endeavours. (Once, my elder son, Josiah, asked me why I wasn't like other daddies who were around most of the time; but after a little reflection he decided firmly that he far preferred a daddy who was on television and in the papers to one who didn't do anything interesting.)

Nor am I able, except very occasionally, to pursue the personal interests that give me pleasure, such as cooking and cleaning – and rearing goats. My greatest passion in life is still academic study and this too is now almost impossible for me. I try to keep abreast of developments in theology and political science, but it has become ever harder to make any real progress and I long for the day when I will be able to return to serious research. Having said that, I rejoice in the fact that the practice of peacemaking has enabled me to develop a level of knowledge and expertise that is beyond the realm of possibility for most academics.

In some ways, my spiritual life has also suffered. I no longer have the privilege of sharing in the daily worship of a beautiful cathedral like Coventry. Instead, I have to make time to find God amidst a chaotic existence in often hostile places. Yet I would say that my experience of God has been deeper than it used to be, because I have not been able to rely on the security of structured prayer and worship but instead have been aware of God's presence in some very adverse situations. Over the past few years my spirituality has had to become more rigorous in many ways in order to survive the many different environments in which I am called to work. I have also had the opportunity to engage with local people of faith whose trust in God has survived the rigours of great suffering. The faces of the worshippers at St George's in Baghdad on a Sunday afternoon always gave me the strength and courage to persevere in the coming week. My sermons became increasingly interactive as I realized that I had as much to gain from the daily experiences of the Christian community as from my understanding of scripture and theology.

Throughout, I have enjoyed the support and encouragement not only of my own diocese and bishop but also of the Bishop of Cyprus and the Gulf, Clive Handford, in whose diocese Iraq lies, and of the community of All Nations Church in Charlotte, North Carolina, and their ministers, Bonnie and Mahesh Chavda. It has been the children of that church and their almost daily e-mails that have encouraged me more than anything else. It has also been good for me to be constantly reminded that I am not in fact a maverick. As a priest in the Anglican communion, I am accountable to God for my actions through my bishop, and the structure and discipline of that church set my work as a peacemaker within the context of my priestly calling.

Issues regarding my health I had initially kept very private until a national newspaper in Britain revealed that I suffer from multiple sclerosis. This has indeed been a great challenge as I face what many regard as one of the most dangerous jobs in the world. Unfortunately, I do not have one of the more benign forms of MS but am daily faced with a barrage of debilitating symptoms of an increasingly progressive disease. It has been faith and hope and the shoulders of my bodyguards that have enabled me to keep going. But my condition deteriorates markedly whenever I stop working and whenever I am cold, and so it would seem that the extreme stress and heat of Baghdad are actually very good for me.

Chapter 3

Hope, edged with fear

With hostilities formally ended, I was desperate to return to Iraq. The retired American general Jay Garner had taken control of the country at the head of the Office of Reconstruction and Humanitarian Assistance (ORHA), but it soon became apparent that big mistakes had been made straight away and after just one month he was replaced by the relatively unknown diplomat Paul Bremer, who had served Ronald Reagan as 'ambassador-at-large for counter-terrorism' in the 1980s. I wanted to see our friends, to assess the damage from the war and to find out what we could now do to help to bring about peace and reconciliation. However, the country was still very unsafe. Looting was rife and there were many vigilante groups in and around the major cities. In particular, the road from Amman to Baghdad was said to be very dangerous.

In early May, Georges decided to go back. He was taking a satellite phone with him, so at least we could be in regular contact with him, and once he reached Jordan we could form a clearer idea of the perils and problems involved in travelling. The cost of getting from Amman to Baghdad had risen from $250 to $2,000 each way, which itself indicated both the danger of the journey and the new demand for access to Iraq. At first, most of those travelling in were journalists; then the relief agencies began to move in. The humanitarian crisis was not as severe as the UN and others had expected: there were only a few thousand refugees if that, rather than up to half a million as the UN had predicted – and most of those were Palestinians who had been living in Iraq. However, in other ways the situation was very bad. The loss of electricity and the damage to water supplies and treatment plants created a serious risk of epidemic. It would take several more weeks to grasp the full extent of the crisis.

After a few days, it seemed safe enough for Georges to return to Iraq. At last we had someone on the ground who could assess the situation and could link up again with our friends and colleagues. He also immediately made contact with the Coalition Provisional Authority (CPA), which had now replaced the short-lived ORHA. As both a Christian and a former senior military officer who had no sympathy with the old regime, he was in a very good position to help the Coalition authorities with the task of reconstruction.

Very little thought had been given by either London or Washington to the matter of 'religious reconstruction', so before I set a date for my return I discussed my concerns in depth with the American State Department and the National Security Council, and with my friend and colleague Dr David Smock of the United States Institute of Peace. David is a leading expert in the field of religion and conflict and we had already worked closely together on several projects. He knew as well as I did that religion can easily be a force for ill as well as for good.

Finally, I spoke several times to the senior British diplomats in the CPA. Particularly helpful was the advice of Major General Tim Cross, the most senior British soldier in the authority. He is a committed Christian and an expert on reconstruction, having gained solid experience in Kosovo. We sat at his kitchen table on his first return to England and discussed our fears. It was obvious that he cared passionately about the future of the Iraqi people. He expressed great concern about the rising religious tensions and said it was important that I and my team should return sooner rather than later. He told me frankly, however, how dangerous Iraq had become and suggested that I go in a week or two, 'when the situation will be under control'.

I decided to return at the end of May, along with my fellow director of the ICR, Canon Justin Welby. Georges' son-in-law Nabil Omiesh would take care of our arrangements in Jordan, as he had done so often before. The desert highway to Baghdad was now so hazardous that most vehicles were travelling in convoy, leaving at set times. Our timings didn't fit in with this schedule, but for an extra $200 we found a driver willing to take us alone.

We set off from Amman at 6 a.m. and by midday had reached the border, where we were joined by other vehicles also making this intrepid journey. Gone were the laborious entry requirements, the hours of waiting, the AIDS tests and the shabbiest VIP lounge in the world, with the duty-free frying pan still unsold. Gone too were the ubiquitous pictures of Saddam. This time, the border control consisted of one American soldier chewing gum with a big smile, and the only question was 'Where are you guys from?' followed by 'Have a nice stay!' And then we were through. We didn't appreciate it then, but we had just witnessed one of the biggest mistakes the Coalition had made. We had got into Iraq with ease – as did many hundreds of others whose intentions were a lot less benign.

Our driver, who spoke little English, kept saying 'Ali Baba! Ali Baba!' We had quickly learned that this was the term used for the bandits on the road, and now we discovered that only last week they had stopped him and taken all his passengers' money and electrical equipment. We promptly hid all our valuables and instructed him to stay with the convoy, and on the most dangerous stretch of road, between Ramadi and Falluja, to drive at at least 110 m.p.h.

Despite the war, the road to Baghdad was undamaged. There was no obvious military presence and the only difference we could see was that there was slightly more traffic. When we got to our destination, however, the change was immediately apparent. Almost every ministry and government building had been destroyed, either by bombing or by fire. The dreaded face of the iron dictator had gone, though the remains of his statues, mosaics and portraits could still be seen. It was an emotional experience, being back in Baghdad. It felt very different. No longer was there a heavy, dark cloud of oppression hanging over the people. There was still great hardship, but now there was a sense of freedom – a freedom that money could not buy, a freedom obtained by sacrifice that was still not understood or appreciated by much of the world.

There was no time for rest or recuperation. Georges had already set up meetings for us with the CPA. We left almost immediately for Saddam's old Republican Palace, a place far removed from the ordinary people that had been a symbol of tyranny and fear and was now the CPA's headquarters. As we drove up to its gates I could see the adjoining palace, where I used to meet with Tariq Aziz, lying in ruins.

Entering Saddam's palace was a surreal experience. It must be strange for everyone working there to be based in the home of one of the cruellest dictators of recent years. For me, having spent so much time with Iraqis and sensed the fear they lived in, it was particularly strange. At the outer gates, we were greeted by young American soldiers, both male and female. They searched every visitor, but not in a horrible, intrusive way. Everything was done in a serious but informal manner. The palace drive, straight and well kept, must be nearly a mile long and there were tanks and other military vehicles parked at intervals along it. Our first glimpse of the Palace itself was of the four huge bronze heads of Saddam that surmounted it. At its entrance we were once again searched, by Gurkhas now working for private security firms. Some 40 of them were based in Baghdad at the time and they were chiefly responsible for guarding the Palace.

We were there to meet General Cross and Britain's 'special representative', John Sawers. The latter was an old friend of mine who as ambassador to Egypt in 2002 had given me crucial help in drafting the Alexandria Declaration – the first joint statement from Christian, Jewish and Muslim leaders from the 'Holy Land', which called for an end to violence and a religiously sanctioned ceasefire – when the whole process was on the verge of collapse. When we saw each other, we embraced, a greeting far more Middle Eastern in style than British Establishment. Meeting him again was an emotional experience for me. Indeed, the whole occasion was very emotive – in this palace, a nation was being rebuilt. General Cross, who shared an office with Mr Sawers, just next door to Paul Bremer, was rather excited. He had just returned from Babylon and he told us of all he had seen as he walked around its ruins with the Bible as his guide. That Bible was open now on his desk and on it lay an old piece of sackcloth and some ashes he had found in a hole in the ground. Who knows how ancient they may have been?

It was a while before we got down to business. The main concern was the involvement of religious leaders in the task of rebuilding Iraq and the reformation of the Ministry of Religious Affairs. We agreed to meet properly the following Monday, but first there was the matter of opening St George's for worship on the Sunday. It was decided that we would have the service at 10 a.m. and that John Sawers and General Cross would each read a lesson.

Before we left, Georges took us on a short tour of the Palace. Most of it is quite magnificent, in the Oriental manner – built of fine brick and stone and finished inside with Italian marble and gleaming crystal chandeliers. It is also huge – it made Buckingham Palace look like a suburban semi. Four thousand people were now working in the building, and most of them also slept there. Not only the rooms but even the corridors were filled with mattresses, computers – and bottles of water. Although the Palace had not been bombed, most of the utilities didn't work and there was no air-conditioning and very little running water, and in the blazing heat of an Iraqi summer one can very quickly get dehydrated. With only irregular electricity from temperamental generators and no internal communication system, everyone was working with laptops and satellite phones. Various rooms were labelled with the name of the department that was headquartered there, and Justin was particularly bemused by a sign that located the Ministry of Justice underneath a flight of stairs.

By the time we left the Palace we were desperate for a shower. Our usual hotel, al-Rashid, being government property had been thoroughly looted and was no longer open, so instead we booked into the Palestine. That hotel had itself been hit by tank fire during the war but it was relatively unharmed and it had a far more pleasant feel than al-Rashid. Here too there was only intermittent water and electricity, but it was clean and certainly more comfortable than the Palace.

In the evening, we went out for dinner to one of my old haunts, a delightful Assyrian restaurant in the centre of the city. It had survived the war unscathed and it was wonderful to see the owners again under such different circumstances. A tank stood on the street outside, and several American soldiers. We got talking to them and heard something of their experience over the past few months. They all said they were homesick and hadn't spoken to their families since they'd said goodbye to them. They looked hungrily at our satellite phone – and how could we refuse them? One of them was in tears as he spoke to his mother, and the joy on all their faces was unforgettable.

The next day we made our way to St George's. Standing between the Ministry of Information and the national theatre, the church had been in a very vulnerable position and yet it was totally undamaged. This was the answer to all those who asked whether the bombing was precise or not. Here we were to have another emotional reunion, with the caretaker and his family. Despite our fears, they had survived the war – but they had not escaped all the trauma that followed it. Hanna had sent his family to stay with relatives but he had remained behind to guard the church and, soon after the war, looters had broken in and tied him up and taken everything in sight. Hanna had few possessions, but over the past four years he had tried very hard to turn the church hall into a comfortable home for his family. Everything was stolen, including the pews and the organ. The only fixture that remained was the solid marble font. The looters even managed to achieve something that had defeated the bishop, which was to retrieve the contents of the safe. When Hanna was discovered and freed after 30 hours, all he could find was a single cross of solid silver, made in England and given in memory of a soldier who fell in the First World War. Who knows why that too wasn't taken?

Georges had told Hanna that a service would be taking place and we found everything ready and in order for worship. A congregation of local people had already gathered, along with most of the British diplomats and several senior members of the American military. As I stood on the church steps welcoming new arrivals, I had a strong sense of the presence of God. In Iraq, we were not just dealing with military and political forces – something profoundly spiritual was also going on here. I became increasingly aware of the security that was surrounding the church. There were tanks and armoured personnel carriers, soldiers on foot and, overhead, as if joining the hosts of angels I certainly hoped were present, Apache helicopters.

Inside the church, the atmosphere was charged. I had taken

many services here before and we had often referred to St George's as 'a broken church in a broken land'. Now things were different. The church was still broken and so was the land, but now for the first time in years there was hope. Hope that very soon Iraq would be a different kind of place, where justice and mercy ruled and freedom was once again known by all.

Justin led the service and I preached the sermon. I chose as my text Haggai 2.9, a verse that had been so important to Coventry Cathedral after the war: '"The glory of this present house will be greater than the glory of the former house," says the LORD Almighty. "And in this place I will grant peace," declares the LORD Almighty.' The Gospel reading was St Matthew's version of the Beatitudes and the psalm was Psalm 137:

> By the rivers of Babylon we sat and wept
> when we remembered Zion.

All three readings were very emotional and evocative in this peculiar setting – an Anglican church in the heart of Baghdad filled with American soldiers, British diplomats and Iraqi Christians and Muslims. And then in the midst of this gathering the Patriarch of the Ancient Church of the East (Old Calendar) turns up. Mar Addai II is one of the most colourful of Iraq's Christian leaders and he obviously thought he should be present at the reopening of a church in his city, even if it was Protestant.

I spoke about God's promise to the people of Israel that they would one day live in peace in their own land, no longer strangers, no longer fearful and no longer without hope. I tried to encourage the local people that a new day had come when they would at last be free. Yet I acknowledged their great suffering, not just in recent months but for many years. I also wanted to address the Coalition forces, who also needed encouragement. I spoke of the high calling of peacemakers, for, as the Beatitudes say, 'they will be called sons of God'. When we came to Communion, everybody came forward, and around our Lord's Table we were reconciled, as children of God from different nations and different backgrounds, and we were one.

After the service we got talking to the many different people present. We heard stories from the Americans, including one of the military commanders who led his troops into Baghdad. We heard of the jubilation that Saddam had finally fallen and we heard of the continued suffering of the ordinary people of Iraq. A Muslim woman who had brought her family to the church told us how they had lost everything, at the hands not of the Coalition but of the looters who had taken advantage of their new freedom. The general feeling though was one of joy and excitement. One woman told me she had attended the church many years ago as a child, and another said that her parents had been married there. Not everyone in the congregation spoke English, but Georges did a brilliant job translating.

Later we made our way through the baking streets to the home of Ayatollah al-Sadr and entered his familiar, high-walled compound for the first time without a minder from the Mukhabarat. Always before in our meetings with the ayatollah we had been watched continuously and notes of our conversation had been openly taken. Now, as I entered the main reception room of the house, it was obvious that things were different. No longer was there the tension and fear I had experienced before. His disciples and his fellow sayeds (like all the ayatollahs, direct descendants of Imam Ali, Mohammed's son-in-law and the founder of Shia Islam) looked relaxed as they strolled around in their large black or white turbans and their flowing blue and black robes.

Eventually, the ayatollah walked in – one of the greatest Shia leaders in the world, a man in whom I had seen such holiness. With arms opened wide he met me in the centre of the room and we embraced. This was no Middle Eastern courtesy, but an expression of genuine love. With tears in our eyes, we held each other tightly for several minutes and then took each other's hand and sat down together. I am not sure what my colleagues made of this show of great affection, but this was our first meeting in freedom and it was a deeply emotional occasion. The ayatollah greeted me with the traditional words of welcome and spoke of his joy – and then said something very true. He declared that even though we could not talk openly in the days of terrible oppression, our spirits had spoken to each other. The love of God that we both had at the centre of our lives meant that we had so much in common we could communicate without words.

After this, we called at a children's home that I used to visit before the war, which had been run by Mother Teresa's Sisters of Charity. (It was just round the corner from the restaurant the Americans had obliterated with four 'bunker-busting' bombs after a tip-off that Saddam was dining there.) The sisters were still there – throughout the war, local people had taken care of them all and made sure they had food and water. I spent some time with the children and then asked about Ahmed and Immanuel, two little boys I had grown especially fond of on my previous visits. Their terrible congenital deformities had made their lives hopeless, but the sisters had rescued them and given them hope. One of the sisters took me into the sitting room and there on the wall were the most wonderful pictures of the boys. A kind-hearted Australian doctor had taken them both back to her country for treatment. There they had undergone extensive surgery and been fitted with state-of-the-art artificial limbs and now they could walk unaided and could even play football. The sisters told me that Saddam's regime had put them under pressure to bring the boys back to Iraq after a year, but they said it is now very unlikely that they will return. I just hope that one day I will have the chance to see them again.

Meanwhile, Ahmed and Immanuel had been replaced by other children who had been born without limbs, and what help would come to them no one knew. The sisters continued to provide outstanding care for their charges. They appeared full of grace but rather tired. I asked them if they ever had any holiday, and they said yes – once every ten years they would go back to India for a little while. Apart from that, they worked all day every day.

The following day, we returned to the Palace for further meetings with John Sawers and General Cross. We discussed in depth the complicated interreligious issues that were now coming to the surface and we talked through possible ways to prevent further conflict. It was obvious that the years of engagement that I and my colleagues had had with the religious leadership of Iraq had equipped us uniquely to deal with some of these problems. So much of this society is based around relationships, and the one thing we had that the Coalition did not was relationships. In Arabic cultures, you have to earn trust and respect.

Before we left our meeting with General Cross for yet further meetings with American diplomats and soldiers, he told us of some rather important intelligence that had come in the previous day. There had been reliable reports that there would be an attempt to blow up St George's during the service. The most senior diplomats and soldiers were informed of this but they all decided that they would still come to worship. This explained the cordon of troops around the church and the Apaches above it. It was the first of many dangerous situations we found ourselves faced with in post-war Iraq.

After a series of intensive meetings, mainly in the Palace with members of the CPA, we drove back to Amman. As we raced to the border on that long desert road, the signal returned to my mobile phone and I called the office of Prince Hassan. The former Crown Prince of Jordan is a very fine man, a scholar and the moderator of the World Conference on Religion and Peace. He is also a very good friend of the former Archbishop of Canterbury, Lord Carey. He told me he was able to see us, and it wasn't long before a car picked us up from our hotel in Amman to take us to his palace for a long and fruitful meeting. The Prince had already gathered some representatives of Iraq's religious leaders in Jordan and he was acutely aware of the potential for interreligious conflict in a country that had once been ruled by his own family.

Back at the hotel, we met with the Bishop, Clive Handford. He had not yet gone back to Iraq himself, but he intended to do so soon and he was obviously eager to know how things were in that part of his vast diocese. We told him about our discussions with the CPA and the possibility of our further involvement, and he encouraged us to persevere.

Once we were back in Britain we were able to weigh our response. If we were going to play a major role in the restoration of Iraq it would have a big impact on our work in other areas. The final decision would be made not by us but by the Archbishop of Canterbury, on whose behalf I was co-ordinating the Alexandria Process, the religious 'track' of the search for peace in Israel/Palestine. In the event, Dr Williams was clear that my priority should be Israel/Palestine and I accepted this, though I said that the ICR at Coventry Cathedral still had to meet its existing commitments in Iraq.

In the next few days I had some other crucial meetings, not least with the Foreign Secretary, Jack Straw, and Baroness Symons, the Minister of State for the Middle East. It was only a matter of weeks since I had received that rather complacent letter from the Foreign Office, and already the realization had dawned that questions of religion were going to be very significant in the rebuilding of Iraq. Even the supplies of water and electricity could not be sorted out without some degree of intercommunal co-operation. The new Iraq was full of hope, but that hope was more than edged with fear. We all knew that things could deteriorate very quickly.

Was the war justified?

All war is dreadful. There are losers on all sides. Death and destruction become the norm. 'Collateral damage' is merely a euphemism for the killing or maiming of real people. Modern technology may try to make war clean, but it can never succeed. The Third Gulf War was no exception. It may have been quick, but it left thousands of people dead or injured. All of us who were involved in Iraq wanted this war to be avoided – for several years I had been working to that very end. When the bombardment began, in the early hours of 20 March 2003, I felt that I had failed.

My mind went back to my last visit to Iraq before the war. I recalled the long-drawn-out meetings with people like Tariq Aziz and the Foreign Minister, Naji Sabri al-Hadithi. It was almost as if they knew war was coming: they pledged to fight hard (though in the event they did not). However, it was not the words of politicians that stayed in my mind but those of ordinary Iraqi people, who pleaded with me that they needed to be liberated from Saddam's regime. They knew that a war would involve great pain, but this time they were prepared to suffer.

In November 2002, I had returned from Baghdad to London, where a major debate on Iraq was to take place in what was the new Archbishop of Canterbury's first General Synod. The last time the subject had been debated I had vehemently opposed both sanctions and any further attacks on Iraq. This time, my position had changed. I passed on the words of the Iraqi people: 'We have had enough.'

Nevertheless, not even the will of the majority of an oppressed nation actually justifies a war of liberation, according to the theory of just war developed by Augustine and Thomas Aquinas. This laid down certain criteria, grouped under three headings:

Ius ad bellum (Justice in going to war)
Ius in bello (Justice in waging war)
Ius post bello (Justice after the war).

We need to consider all these criteria if we are to establish whether a third Gulf War was justified or not. What follows here is no more than my own personal assessment, based on my experiences in Iraq before and after the war. This has been by far the most difficult part of this book to write. There are days when I feel that my judgement is wrong, but I have tried to present the balance of my opinion on this difficult theological, philosophical and political issue.

Ius ad bellum (Justice in going to war)
Was it right to go to war against Saddam Hussein? This has been one of the biggest questions posed since the war. Many people believed that his possession of 'weapons of mass destruction' (WMDs) was the principal reason for the war. Although none was ever found, the intelligence for their existence was very strong – and it remains strong, as many, many people tell of their own roles in helping to conceal these weapons. I don't understand why these stories, too numerous to be merely inventions, have not been related by the media. Nor do I understand why the countless accounts of people being injured and even killed while moving these weapons have not been reported. In reality, much of the experience of the people of Iraq has yet to be told – though elsewhere in this book I tell something of the torture and murder that came to light once the country was liberated.

According to just-war theory, to justify war there have to be:

- a *just cause* – to prevent an attack or to correct grave injustice;
- a *competent authority* to sanction the war;

- *limited objectives*, and a *reasonable hope of success*;
- *right intention*, without ulterior motives.

Moreover, war must always be a *last resort*.

Just cause

When I last visited Iraq before the Coalition invaded, it was obvious that the suffering of the Iraqi people was so immense that they saw no way out without war. Yet the reasons commonly put forward to justify the war were concerned not with the Iraqi people but with the threat Saddam posed to the rest of the world. For me it was the welfare of ordinary Iraqis that was paramount, but I have no doubt that Saddam was indeed a danger that had to be dealt with. The fact that no WMDs were found does not mean that they didn't exist: we know that Saddam had them in the 1980s, when he used them to massacre thousands of Iraqis. Therefore the criterion of a just cause was almost certainly fulfilled.

Competent authority

Sanction by a competent authority is a more difficult matter. Many governments deplored the fact that the UN Security Council did not categorically authorize the war. The majority of its 15 members evidently did not feel that sufficient time had been given to the weapons inspectors to establish whether or not Saddam still possessed WMDs, and as a result a resolution that actually authorized war was never put to the vote, let alone passed. But is the UN the only authority competent to sanction a war? This question is widely debated in political, legal and theological circles. It is a fact that the UN has lost much of its political authority in recent years, to some extent because most of the Arab nations have been voting *en bloc*.

Despite the lack of UN approval, the war had the backing not only of America and Britain but of over 40 other states, including most of those adjoining Iraq. This point must be taken seriously and cannot be ignored. America did not go to war unilaterally, though much of the world accused it of doing so. The Coalition supporting the war in Iraq can therefore be said to have had competent authority even without the sanction of the UN.

Limited objectives

Public statements from Washington and London in the build-up to the war disagreed about what its objectives might be. Both governments spoke of the need to remove the threat of WMDs, but the Americans were not coy about saying that they would also like to remove Saddam. Certainly, if there was real concern for the Iraqi people – and I think that in some quarters there was – it was essential that the primary cause of their suffering should be dealt with. This indeed was achieved, far earlier than expected, when Baghdad fell on 9 April 2003 and the tyrant was toppled once and for all. Fifteen months later – despite attempts by some, both in America and in Iraq, to prolong the role of the Coalition's chief administrator, Paul Bremer – sovereignty was handed over to the Iraqi people and from that day on their interim government had real authority. Thus, the war can be seen to have had limited objectives.

Reasonable hope of success

This is by far the easiest of the six criteria to satisfy. There was never any serious doubt that the Coalition would be victorious.

Right intention

If a war is to be judged just, it must seek to restore a just peace without ulterior motives. Many people have claimed that the war was really all about Iraq's vast oil reserves. I do not believe this to be true. It would take many, many generations before America could even begin to recoup the huge financial resources it has put into Iraq. Billions of dollars have been invested not only in fighting the war and in maintaining security subsequently but also in restoring the country's infrastructure. A stronger claim could be made for the geopolitical objective of having a presence in Iraq at the heart of the Arab world. Yet America already had a stronghold in Saudi Arabia, arguably the most powerful and most significant Arab state. I personally believe that the intention to go to war against Iraq was right, even though I have reservations about the 'threat' that Iraq posed to the Western world.

Last resort

In February 2003, Tony Blair declared in the House of Commons that the Iraqi people had suffered enough. Nearly 13 years of sanctions on top of the terrible abuse inflicted by Saddam had indeed traumatized the nation. It can be clearly argued that the methods the West and the UN had used to try to control him had failed dismally. The population of Iraq had been brought to its knees while the tyrant and his family lived in increasing luxury. There is no doubt that going to war against Saddam was a last resort. Indeed, it can be argued that we tolerated his regime for too long, resulting in the suffering and death of millions.

To my mind, therefore, the first six criteria, of *ius ad bellum*, were clearly met.

Ius in bello (Justice in waging war)

Was the war fought justly? According to just-war theory, there are two conditions: *proportionality* and *discrimination*. These are much easier to deal with.

Proportionality

Despite the language of 'shock and awe', it was clear that the assault on Iraq was largely aimed at the government and the armed forces. There were very few attacks on the rest of the country's infrastructure – in contrast to the Second Gulf War in 1991, when (for example) vital bridges, power plants and sewage works were bombed. Some of the destruction of that earlier war was still apparent on my first visit to Iraq eight years later. The damage done in the Third Gulf War will be much more quickly made good.

Discrimination

As one drives around Iraq, and in particular Baghdad, the evidence of war is obvious. In the capital, almost every government building was destroyed – and yet the buildings next door are generally untouched. A typical example is our own church of St George in the heart of the city. On one side are the shattered remains of the Ministry of Information and on the other are the ruins of the national theatre, yet between them the church still stands – totally wrecked by the looters but unscathed by the bombing. This story was repeated throughout Baghdad.

There were, of course, exceptions – sometimes buildings were bombed by accident or as a result of faulty intelligence, such as the restaurant in al-Mansur where Saddam was believed to be dining. That particular attack resulted in the deaths of a number of innocent people, both Muslim and Christian, including several children. And yet, despite such tragedies, the 'collateral damage' was truly minimal.

It is, I therefore believe, fair to say that the force the Coalition used to gain victory was indeed proportionate and was applied with discrimination.

Ius post bello (Justice after the war)

The final criterion for a just war is the most difficult to satisfy. It has been widely acknowledged that the Coalition made some grave mistakes, which arose not least from a failure to understand Iraqi society and its ethnic, religious and cultural diversity. Two principal errors made it particularly difficult to maintain order after the war and ensure a smooth transition to democracy. The first of these was the failure to secure the country's borders. The second was the immediate dismissal of all of Iraq's security forces, including the police, the army and the intelligence services. Clearly, some people had to go, but the result of sacking everyone was the anger and anarchy that engulfed the nation. Mistakes are still being made, not only by the Coalition forces but also by the interim government. This is not surprising, as Iraq is a large country being run by people of relatively little experience. Governing a society as diverse as this is not easy. Nonetheless, having worked closely with the CPA, the various embassies and the multinational forces, I am convinced that they all have worked extremely hard to restore order, repair the infrastructure and return power to the Iraqi people as quickly as possible. The Pentagon especially has made every effort to put things right.

My own conclusion is that in every respect the Third Gulf War met the criteria of classical just-war theory. This does not mean that I am in favour of war – on the contrary, I deplore it. The truth is that we should never go to war unless it is worse not to. From my experience of pre-war Iraq, I can say without a shadow of a doubt that it would have been worse not to have gone to war.

Chapter 4

The tale of suffering

I was back in Baghdad just three weeks later. There was the usual round of meetings with representatives of the Coalition (though this time we were concentrating on the Americans) and I continued to call on the many religious leaders I had got to know and respect over the years. The only people I couldn't see were Sheikh Dr Abdel Latif Humayem, who had fled Iraq immediately after the war, and the Chaldean patriarch, Raphael I Bidawid, who was seriously ill in a Lebanese hospital.

The increasing heat was making the Palace unbearable. The temperature inside the building was over 45°C, and most of the thousands of staff who were working there (and the hundreds still sleeping there) were not convinced by assurances that the air-conditioning would soon be working. It was not the best environment for stressful work.

A chapel had been set up at the Palace – as it happened, in Saddam's throne-room, which was central and an appropriate size – and on the Sunday morning I was asked to preach there. The readings for the day were from the end of Job and the prologue of John's Gospel, and 2 Corinthians 5.11–17. There could not have been better readings to speak on in this surreal atmosphere. There were about 70 people present at the 7.30 a.m. service, a mixture of soldiers and diplomats. I talked a little about my involvement in Iraq over the past four years but I focused on the theme of reconciliation and the fact that everyone present was involved in the work of bringing peace and healing, which was the work of the Kingdom of God. I spoke of the anguish of the Iraqi people and of their courage over the years, but I did not ignore the suffering too of those present. Several had lost friends and colleagues in the war and many were feeling the heartache of several months' separation from their loved ones. To them the words of Job to God spoke clearly: 'My ears had heard of you but now my eyes have seen you.'

After the service, I had breakfast with Georges in the Palace restaurant. We were in the heart of the Middle East and yet, with a menu of 'grits', biscuit and gravy, and pancakes and syrup, it was a meal that could have been served in any city in the southern States. The only thing unAmerican about the experience was the people serving the food, who were mainly from south Asia. It was as if Tennessee had been transported in to the Palace. After we'd eaten, there was just time for a quick meeting with John Sawers before I returned to St George's to lead the morning worship. I had brought with me two chalices and pattens from Jerusalem, made in an Armenian pottery there – something one would never have dared do under the old regime. The service was well attended, this time mainly by Iraqis.

As soon as it was over, we made our way to the home of Ayatollah al-Sadr. His house was particularly crowded that day, as there were a large number of people hoping to see him. The 90 minutes we spent waiting for him were among the most chilling of my life. Sitting with us in the 'saloon' were several members of the ayatollah's family as well as students from his seminary, and they told us their stories of what they and he had suffered under Saddam.

The ayatollah had been imprisoned 18 times for long periods, and more briefly too many times to count. The young imams related a litany of torture. They told us how the ayatollah had often been hung by his feet for hours from a fan-like construction that continuously rotated. Suddenly I remembered the pain in his knees that he used to complain of when he was in England, and how I had had to take him to see a doctor. Then they told us how they themselves had been stood under dripping water and beaten with live wires, how they had been incarcerated underground in rat-infested cells and even buried alive in coffins for days at a time. They told us of the instruments of torture that were used on them, all made in the USA or in Belgium – apart from the surgical instruments that were used to remove their finger- and toe-nails, which were made in Britain. So far the young imams spoke frankly and without any sign of distress, and at times they even laughed, especially when they mentioned where the instruments of torture came from. But then their manner changed as they spoke of what had been done to their wives and children.

The atrocities committed by Saddam's evil regime are well known, but to hear at first hand of the sheer terror people endured at the hands of his henchmen was at times almost too awful to bear. The litany continued. 'If we didn't return on time from a trip, our wives would be taken into prison and raped and tortured.' 'And your children?' I asked. 'When one of our brothers was late back from Syria,' they told me, 'the whole family were taken and in front of them all a three-year-old boy was picked up by his ankles and his head was smashed against the wall until his brains came out.'

A deathly silence fell over the room. What do you say when you hear of such wickedness? Tears filled my eyes as the tale of suffering continued. Most of the stories I heard that day are too horrible to repeat. It would feel almost as if you were adding to their degradation if you repeated such things. I asked myself the question: Should I ever have dealt with such a dreadful regime? But whenever I asked that question of Shia leaders and others who had suffered much, their answer was always 'Yes'. They said that for some years I had been their only friend from the outside world. They knew that I was aware of their suffering, even if I had no idea of its severity.

Eventually the ayatollah arrived, for yet another emotional reunion. This time we ate together, a huge feast of all my favourite Iraqi food – *mansaf, qorsi* and *masguf,* a very large fish that is cooked beside an open fire. We spoke of our plans, of how we now needed to work very closely together to try to build a new Iraq where tolerance and kindness reigned instead of death and destruction. I was now more than ever convinced that the war had been necessary. Even if no WMDs had been found, the most terrible weapon of mass destruction had been Saddam himself. He had been responsible for the deaths of hundreds of thousands of people – the whole story will never be told because entire families and tribes were wiped out. It was not only the Shia, the Kurds, the Marsh Arabs and opponents of the regime who suffered. Even those who held senior positions in the government, the civil service and the armed forces were at risk. Everyone was one step away from torture or execution. Everyone was a potential victim.

Later that evening, driving through the streets of Baghdad, Georges pointed out one of the many bombed ministries. He explained that this had been where Saddam's son Uday had run his Olympics Committee office. Wherever Uday was, there was evil. Georges went on to tell us that he himself had been imprisoned in this building for nine months after the Second Gulf War. He had been recalled to the airforce to take charge of the British, American and Kuwaiti prisoners of war – but then had received a direct order from Uday to have them killed. When he refused, he was promptly dismissed – and once the war had ended, the Mukhabarat came for him. But he was fortunate: he could easily have been executed himself.

The father of our driver, Nashwan, was also a general and a

friend and colleague of Georges. He too had been tortured by the regime as a punishment for not carrying out its instructions. He too had got off lightly: he had just had one eye gouged out.

To all the tragedies of the past were now being added new ones. War and its aftermath always produce innocent victims and often these are children, and in the new Iraq there were many now living on the streets. Under the old regime, such a thing would not be permitted and there were a great many state-run institutions for children. Most of these were looted after the war, like most government buildings, and their former inmates now congregate near hotels so they can beg from foreign workers. One morning, I looked out of my hotel window to see small children sleeping around each of the armoured vehicles outside. They were staying close to the soldiers for protection, and later in the day I would see them eating US Army rations.

Two of these boys were always waiting for me by the hotel. They were called Ahmed and Mohammed and they said they were 12, though they looked about eight or nine. One day I asked them to join us for dinner at the Sheraton. The hotel staff objected strongly, but a few stern words and a small bribe were enough to change their minds, and it was very gratifying to watch the boys eat and eat and eat.

These two and another small boy, Laith, soon became very good friends of ours. As the security situation deteriorated they were moved further and further away from the hotels, but still we would take them out to a local restaurant every evening, and whenever I had to leave Baghdad I would pay its owner to feed them until my next visit. As time went by, more and more children would join these dinner parties. The plight of these dear children became an increasing concern for me, and in the end we set up a fund to help them. This enables us to provide them with food, clothes and medicine, though there is still the major problem of finding them a home. The funds that are now required for that are huge. Before the war, one could buy a large villa for $40,000 or rent one for $50 a month. Today, such properties cost several hundred thousand dollars and the rent is in the region of $2,000 a month.

It was certainly a privilege to have these three boys to care for in Baghdad. I asked them once if they knew my name. 'Of course we do,' they replied. 'It is *Baba*' – which means 'Daddy' in Arabic. When I took some pictures of them home to my own little boys, Josiah and Jacob, they wanted to know when they'd be moving in to live with us. Oh, how I wished they could have! But I knew it was impossible, and I knew how traumatic it is when such children are transplanted to an alien culture. Eventually we found a very poor-quality house where they could stay through the winter, and I hoped and prayed that before too long they would have a proper home.

Many other people tried to help them, most of them acting on their own initiative. One was an Italian man living in London called Salvatore Santoro, who said he had made a lot of money and wanted to give it back to God. Later, in December 2004, he would insist on driving to Ramadi in his Porsche. We strongly advised him not to do so, and were saddened but not surprised when we heard that he had been kidnapped and killed.

The US Army did what they could to care for the children, but they were soldiers, not social workers. Talking to them gave us further insights into the dangerous life the children lived on the streets. Most of them were addicted to drugs or sniffed glue. The younger ones were regularly abused by the older boys. The very few girls were often raped, and some were pregnant. Even as we were listening to these stories, a sudden fight broke out. One of the older boys was attacking the younger ones and stealing from them. The soldiers responded quickly, but he put up a very good fight and at one point got away from them. They pointed their rifles at him – not that they were going to shoot him, they were simply using their target lights as torches. In the end, he was captured and handcuffed. His pockets were emptied of bags of glue, which were set on fire, and he was 'taken off to the compound'. But the soldiers knew he would be back in a few days.

Eventually, most of these boys were placed in a home by one of the Shia seminaries. There was, however, one boy left – a Christian called David (or, in Arabic, Dawoud), whose father had been killed by Saddam. He was by far the cleverest of them all. He already spoke Aramaic, Kurdish and Arabic and within three months he had also learned English and Spanish from the soldiers and was translating for them. Initially he slept by the tanks, but after a while he moved into a room with the sniffer dogs in the basement of the Sheraton. Over the months he grew closer to our team and eventually, when we got our own centre, he moved in with us and became part of our family and adopted me as his father.

The tragedy of homeless children was only one consequence of the war, but daily we were distressed with stories of the suffering the Ba'thists had inflicted. Iraq may not have been in the news every day, but it was becoming clear that every day hundreds of people had been massacred by the regime. People would tell us, with tears in their eyes, of their own persecution or the death of their loved ones. Many of these accounts are just too horrific to repeat – but one day the full tale will be told: the story of what was done in every village, town and city in Iraq, of how people were made to suffer before they were put into the mass graves.

On one occasion, I went to meet Yonadam Kana of the Assyrian Democratic Movement. He was the sole Christian on Iraq's new Governing Council and was to become a close colleague. His new offices had previously been the headquarters of Saddam's son Uday, and round the back were the torture chambers. They spoke of the evil of the old regime. Some of these rooms were painted red, and were even lit with red light bulbs, to hide the blood that still flecked the walls; and in the centre of each there was a drain so that the life force of the victims could flow away. Yonadam had found there three swords bearing Saddam's initials, which apparently the tyrant had used to cut people's heads off himself.

This was the reality we saw in those early days after the war: the legacy of the brutality, the suffering, the destruction of human lives. It must not be forgotten. For years, I had been visiting this country, and even those close to me, like Georges, had been too afraid to tell me the full story of the terror they lived under. Now the fear of the state had gone, and slowly people were rebuilding their lives. But soon a new horror was to emerge, which was in its way as terrible as what had gone before: the horror of the insurgency.

Moreover, the CPA had made the two fatal mistakes of dismissing the army and the police – which turned Iraq's security forces at one stroke into a huge pool of angry and unemployed men – and failing to secure the borders. A variety of extremists soon infiltrated the country, including both members of Sunni Wahhabi groups such as al-Qa'ida and militant Shia from Syria and Iran. I had been horrified to meet three young British Asians on the border with Jordan, who told me they had come 'to fight the Coalition'. It was no real surprise when President Bush declared that the 'front line' in 'the war on terror' was now Iraq.

Even so, nobody was quite prepared for the horrendous bombing of the Jordanian embassy on 7 August 2003, when at least 11 people were killed by a huge car bomb. It is not difficult to understand the choice of target. Stuck in-between Iraq and Israel, Jordan had always been in a very difficult position. With no natural resources of its own, it relied on Iraqi oil and in return it acted in effect as a lifeline for the Iraqis throughout the UN sanctions. At the same time, however, it enjoyed a good relationship with Israel and was a close ally of the West, and not least America and Britain.

Worse was to come. I was in Jerusalem on 19 August when I received a call from Georges to say that there had been a colossal explosion at the old Canal Hotel in Baghdad, which was now the local headquarters of the UN. I had spent many hours there over the past few years and it was there that people such as Hans von Sponeck and his predecessor, Dennis Halliday, had been based. The current head of the UN mission was Sergio Vieira de Mello, a seasoned diplomat who was very highly regarded and a real expert in post-war reconstruction. The news was not good. Georges' brother had been working in the building when the bomb went off and he was still missing; and it was thought that Sergio was very badly injured. Half an hour later, Georges phoned again. There was good news and very bad news. His brother was alive, but Sergio was dead.

The world was shocked at this turn of events. If the UN was not safe, who or what was? And why the UN anyway? The answer to that was not so difficult for those of us who had worked in the country before the war. Despite the work of advocates for the Iraqi people like Mr Halliday and Count von Sponeck, the letters 'UN' were always associated with the dreaded word 'sanctions'. It was the UN sanctions that, rightly or wrongly, were seen as the cause of the suffering of the past 13 years. Now somebody had got their revenge. It was certainly a considerable reverse. The UN announced that it was scaling down its operations in Iraq immediately and the NGOs too started saying that they would have to pull all their foreign staff out of the country. The British vacated their recently opened embassy in Baghdad and moved inside the Green Zone.

Worse was yet to come, however. On 29 August, as Ayatollah Mohammed Baqr al-Hakim was leaving the most holy shrine of Imam Ali in Najaf, a huge car bomb was detonated and he and more than a hundred others were killed. The ayatollah, who was head of the Supreme Council for the Islamic Revolution in Iraq, had been the most senior Shia leader living in exile in Iran. His return to Najaf after the war had been greeted with much jubilation by his devoted following, though others had been apprehensive about how he would use his influence.

We had our own encounter with the new lawlessness in July, on the ever more dangerous road between Amman and Baghdad. I had visited Iraq for the first time with our new Middle East project officer, Oliver Scutt, a fine young man who had joined us after working as a researcher for a Member of Parliament. On our return, we left the Palestine Hotel at 5.30 a.m., 30 minutes after the curfew ended, and on the edge of Baghdad met up with the four other cars that would make up our convoy. Once we hit the desert road I settled down to catch up on some sleep, flat out on one of the back seats of our big GMC Suburban. It could only have been half an hour later, as we were racing along the six-lane highway between Falluja and Ramadi at 100 m.p.h., that I was woken by the sound of automatic gunfire. We slammed to a halt. Through the front windscreen I could see two cars, a BMW and a Mercedes Benz, blocking the road. I sat up abruptly and found a Kalashnikov pointing at my head. Oliver shouted to the driver to drive quickly, but he was too sensible to obey. We had encountered Ali Babas on this road before. We knew there was no point trying to escape or play the hero.

There must have been at least seven gunmen, and they wanted money – and lots of it. The rule of the road is a thousand dollars a life. I should not have had much money on me after a week in Baghdad, but we had been given a donation from All Nations Church in Charlotte, North Carolina – a contribution towards the costs both of housing the street children and of getting the bone marrow transplant centre working again – and so I happened to have $3,000 on me in cash. All I could see was the piercing green eyes of the bandit who had his gun trained on me – his head was swathed in a *kafiya*, an Arab head-dress. 'Money, money!' he was shouting. I reached into my wallet and pulled out the 30 crisp hundred-dollar bills. The driver had already handed over all the money he had, including the $350 fare we had already paid him. The bandit snatched the notes and slowly backed away, still pointing his Kalashnikov at us. Within a few minutes, the Ali Babas had crossed the road and driven off back towards Falluja.

Before we had left Baghdad we had asked God to send his angels to protect us on our journey, and he had indeed kept us safe – but the experience had brought home to us the fact that we were on a very dangerous mission and we were certainly a little shaken. The vehicle in front of ours was carrying a team from the *New York Times*, including its foreign-affairs columnist, Thomas L. Friedman. When I met him again, in January 2005 at the World Economic Forum in Davos, I found that I had an instant rapport with him. When you've been held up together at gunpoint, it creates a certain bond.

When I next visited Iraq, in October, exactly six months had elapsed since the capture of Baghdad and the toppling of Saddam's statue. The violence was now worse than ever. The three protected hotels outside the Green Zone – the Sheraton, the Palestine and the Baghdad – were now more like prisons than anything else. They were encircled by huge concrete barriers and the neighbouring roads were closed to traffic. American soldiers were still in overall charge of their security, but they were also guarded by members of the new Iraqi police force as well as by private security men. Inside the hotels there were Gurkhas armed with automatic weapons.

The tension in Baghdad was particularly bad after the arrest of two Islamic clerics. When a crowd of protesters marched to the Palace, a CPA official came out to explain that the arrests had been made by the Iraqi police and not on the instructions of the authority. Within hours, a large car bomb went off outside a police station in the centre of the city, killing several policemen and injuring many other people. It was clear that the police were now a target for insurgents.

We stayed as usual at the Palestine, because we knew the staff and it was central and close to where the street children lived. Many of the CPA staff lived at al-Rashid, but although it was inside the Green Zone it was an easy target, and after a missile attack several of them had moved to the Palestine. Next door, the Baghdad was home to various Americans, including many agents of the CIA, and members of the new, Coalition-appointed

Iraqi Governing Council. Our friend and colleague Mowaffak al-Rubaie also lived there. Whenever we went to visit him it was always hard work getting through the security, and so we were surprised when at midday on Sunday 12 October two suicide car bombers attacked his hotel. The first we knew that something was wrong was when the air filled with putrid black smoke, far worse than the normal Baghdad smog. Six security guards were killed and many people were injured, including Dr Mowaffak. Once again we were very close to danger and yet escaped unscathed.

The latter part of October proved to be even more violent. Missiles were fired at al-Rashid, killing an American colonel as well as a number of Iraqis. At the time, the American Deputy Secretary of Defense, Paul Wolfowitz, was staying there. Then there was the major attack on the headquarters of the International Committee of the Red Cross, very close by our hotel, which left at least 12 people dead. The following week, both the UN and the ICRC announced that they were pulling all but the most essential of their foreign staff out of the country. A deadly alliance seemed to have formed between the hard core of Saddam's Fedayin and the various Islamic militant groups, both Sunni and Shia. And yet, in spite of the fury of their attacks, the great majority of Iraq's religious leaders were committed to trying to create a new Iraq that would be not just free from the tyranny of the last 35 years but free, too, from fear.

From now on we flew into Baghdad, travelling in a 12-seater Air Serve plane that provided a daily taxi service for staff of the CPA and the NGOs. As we prepared for take-off in Amman the pilot would inform us that due to the risk of attack by surface-to-air missiles we would be doing a corkscrew landing at 45 degrees. Nobody on the plane ever seemed at all fazed by this announcement – all of us were in and out of Iraq all the time and we knew how hazardous it was. The landing was certainly an experience, more like a white-knuckle ride at Disneyland than a journey to work. We would circle for 15 minutes before making a sudden steep descent. Taking off from Baghdad was similarly dramatic. The danger of flying over Iraq was demonstrated on 2 November when a Chinook helicopter was shot down over Falluja at the cost of 15 American lives. It was the heaviest loss by the military to date since the formal end of the war.

In the same month, a day before we checked in to it, the Palestine was hit by a rocket, as was the Sheraton next door. This time, the missiles were launched from a donkey-drawn cart. Now, even the most innocuous things were being used in the battle against change.

In the new year, we were back in Baghdad and as usual I was due to preach at the early-morning service in the Palace. When we arrived at the Palace gates at about 7.15 a.m., there was already a long queue of Iraqi workers waiting to get in. Forty-five minutes later, I had just finished my sermon when there was a huge explosion that shook the whole building. The bang was so loud that it sounded as if it was actually inside the Palace. The marines who were in the congregation ran out immediately, but we continued the service and so it was only later that we learned of the magnitude of what had happened.

In the middle of the line of cars waiting to enter the Palace there had been one packed with 1,000 lb of explosives. The bomber had detonated this at the busiest time of the day, killing himself and 22 other people. Most of the dead were Iraqis who were working with the Coalition, but there were several Assyrian Christians among them – members of a community with which we have particularly close relations – including two young women who had been regular worshippers in the chapel. Two American civilians were also killed, and many more were injured. The heat had been so intense that car doors were welded shut and people were burnt to death in their vehicles. The scene was one of complete carnage. The fact that one of my project officers and my new driver, Samir, had been at the spot just minutes before brought home to us once again the reality of the danger we were working in.

By now, we were constantly queueing at checkpoints as we shuttled between the diplomats in the Green Zone and the various religious leaders who lived outside it. The American soldiers were often scared and they would harshly abuse us and threaten us if we didn't follow the procedure exactly. Several times we came very close to being shot by them. As we drove around Baghdad we also came under fire from insurgents and we had many narrow escapes from car bombs. We had 24-hour protection, and it was impossible for me to leave the house without a screen of armed guards. For the first time ever in Iraq, I often felt afraid. My colleagues liked to remind me of an occasion just after the war when the roads in central Baghdad were so jammed I got out of our car and started directing the traffic. I knew that if I was to try such a thing now I would be killed.

There had been a brief lull in the violence after the capture of Saddam back in December, but now the city was once again gripped by fear. The insurgency was growing ever more bloody. Suicide bombers were now taking a daily toll of dead and injured. The streets were often empty and every vehicle was an object of suspicion. It wasn't long before the Coalition's losses since the fall of Saddam exceeded those of the actual war. How many Iraqis were now dead, no one knew.

Who are the insurgents?

It cannot be denied that Iraq is caught in a very dangerous cycle of violence – a cycle that is based on the bizarre philosophy that if I hurt you enough, you will stop hurting me. In simple terms, on one side are the Coalition forces, along with those of the interim government. On the other side, the so-called insurgents are a mixture of Islamists, Sunna and Shia, as well as renegade Ba'thists who oppose the presence of the occupying forces and the installation of the new government.

The violence started with attacks on the Coalition and the interim government and went on to target any Iraqi who was associated with the movement for change. The great majority of those killed or injured are Iraqis – ordinary people, many of whom are working for the Iraqi government simply because they are seeking to avoid another downward spiral, into poverty. Many of those who have joined the army or the police did not really want to. They are doing these jobs because they need to provide for their families.

The Coalition forces and the Iraqi security forces are widely regarded as 'the good guys'. Yet many Iraqis, and indeed many of Iraq's neighbours, see the foreign troops as imperialists who have come to an Islamic land to destroy Islamic standards and the Muslim way of life – and the Iraqi forces are their accomplices. But the opposition is not even as simple as that. Walking one day by the square where Saddam's statue was famously pulled down, I suddenly found myself faced by at least a hundred thousand demonstrators chanting, 'Death to Saddam! Death to the Governing Council! Death to America!' They wanted to be liberated but not occupied.

The opposition does not consist just of people who are shouting for Saddam's return. Most of them do not want that.

The fact is that many Iraqis had unreal expectations of what would follow the fall of the old regime. They imagined that overnight the country would become as affluent and advanced as the Gulf states and that the next day they would be running it themselves. It is also a fact that many Iraqis have suffered at the hands of the Coalition and its forces, not just in such high-profile abuses as those that took place in Abu Ghraib but also in so-called collateral damage, the loss of utilities, the breakdown of law and order and the continuing assaults in the province of al-Anbar, most notably in the city of Falluja, and other areas regarded as troublesome.

Some of the roots of this violence go beyond Iraq, however. The clash between the West and the Islamic world is also a major cause. The atrocities of '9/11' were not entirely unprovoked. One grievance was the presence of 'infidel' American troops on the holy soil of Saudi Arabia, which is anathema to strict Muslims. Another is the apparently blind support that America gives to Israel at the expense of the suffering Palestinians. Another issue is the perceived immorality of the West, which is seen as the rotten fruit of Christian liberalism. (Often it is only the most negative aspects of Christianity that are known in the Muslim world. The controversy over gay bishops in America, for example, has made a big impression.)

Then there is the issue of the supposed decline of Islam that many scholars would trace back to a 12 September. On that day in 1683, at the Battle of Vienna, John III Sobieski finally saw off the Ottoman Turks who had threatened Christian Europe for two-and-a-half centuries. Many Muslims are conscious of moral decay in Islamic countries such as Egypt – and indeed, since the overthrow of Saddam, Iraq.

Broadly speaking, there are three main groups involved in insurgency (though there are many subdivisions within each of these): Sunni radicals, supporters of the old Ba'thist regime and Shia militants. Over the months, each has become increasingly well organized, especially in terms of co-ordinating several simultaneous attacks.

The Sunna are the most numerous and the best organized. They have some links with the former Ba'thists, but their religious commitment is far stronger. Among them there are those who are connected with al-Qa'ida, such as the members of al-Tawhid wa'al-Jihad ('Unity and Struggle'). This particular group is headed by the Jordanian Abu Musab al-Zarqawi, who was appointed by Osama bin Laden as one of the 'emirs', or princes, of al-Qa'ida. In the north, there are other groups of Sunni militants associated with al-Qa'ida, including Ansar al-Islam and Ansar al-Sunna, which have connections with the radical Wahhabi and Salafi movements in neighbouring countries. Indeed, much of their finance comes from Syria and Saudi Arabia and the other Gulf states.

Their principal purpose is to resist Western, and especially American, imperialism. Many of their foreign fighters were previously active in Afghanistan and have simply moved their operations westwards to a theatre of war where they think they will have more success. As well as the Coalition, they also target the Shia majority, who they regard both as having adulterated Islam and as being too close to their arch enemies, the more militant Shia of Iran. Many Iraqi Shia have been assassinated or maimed by Sunni radicals, apparently in an attempt to ignite sectarian conflict between the two religious communities. The Sunni violence has in some ways escalated since the assault by the American troops on Falluja in the late autumn of 2004, which displaced many insurgents to the towns of Mahmudiya, al-Latifiya and al-Hasswa, as well as to Baghdad and to Mosul in the north.

Many of the Ba'th Party's activists were Sunna but there were many other religious and ethnic groups represented in its membership. Not all former Ba'thists by any means are involved in insurgency – indeed, some of my best friends today are former Ba'thists – but most of those that are, are people who have lost the positions and privileges they enjoyed under Saddam and now feel they have been disenfranchised. Most of those now causing trouble are from the west of Iraq, where many were previously involved in smuggling and other illegal activities with the support of the old regime.

Though essentially secular, the former Ba'thists have worked closely with the various Sunni groups. They have considerable funding, from the UAE, Saudi Arabia, Syria and Iran, and their aim appears to be to cause as much havoc as possible in the interim government and among those who work with it and for the Coalition. Although the old regime did not export terrorism, it did institutionalize terror, and many of the people now involved in insurgency were previously involved in repression. In particular, some of the old Mukhabarat are active in these groups. A worrying development is the increasing evidence of collaboration between them – and, to a lesser extent, some of the Sunni groups – and Iraq's new security services.

Despite initial fears in the West, it has become obvious that Iraq's Shia majority is much less inclined towards radicalism than their co-religionists in Iran. Most of their leaders are in fact extremely moderate. Indeed, although Islam does not encourage its adherents to 'turn the other cheek', the severe persecution of the Shia under Saddam has taught them to accept suffering as part of the struggle towards freedom, and they are for that reason much less likely than the Sunna to be provoked into violence.

There are, however, some who are more extreme, of whom the most radical is Muqtada al-Sadr, a young cleric who has considerable influence because of his father, a grand ayatollah killed by Saddam. He has assembled a paramilitary force known as the 'Mehdi Army', and has also gathered around him former Ba'thists and others who feel marginalized in the new Iraq. He has won support especially in the south of Iraq and in the poor suburb of Baghdad once called 'Saddam City' but now renamed 'Sadr City' after his father.

The Shia militants are known to receive funding from Iran, which (like other neighbours of Iraq) feels threatened by the idea of a democracy next door and also wants to make trouble for the West. The influence of the eminent Grand Ayatollah Ali Sistani has for the most part greatly reduced their activity, but a recent worrying development has been an effectual – and extraordinary – alliance between some Sunni militants and the followers of Muqtada al-Sadr.

It has been estimated that there are more than 200,000 people involved in insurgency in Iraq, but it is important to note that many of them are doing it because they are paid to. The great majority are young men without jobs and without status who have hired out their services – and hired them out rather than sold them. We know from experience that if you offer them more money they will change sides and become peacemakers. Only the really serious players are committed to their particular cause.

While it is not acceptable to deal directly with terrorists, there has to be some negotiation, and even compromise, with the insurgents if there is going to be any hope of stopping a cycle of violence that could well lead to civil war. Military power alone is not enough. There are those who have access to these people and some influence over them, and we have to talk to them.

Chapter 6

The pursuit of peace

It was clear that if we were to make any real progress in the search for peace it was no longer enough to visit the religious leaders; we needed to get them involved in something organized. Ayatollah al-Sadr had already made known his desire for the establishment of an Institute of Religious Tolerance, and the idea was being widely discussed.

An endless source of help was Christopher Segar, a seasoned diplomat fluent in Arabic who in May 2003 had been appointed head of the new *de facto* British embassy. He had served in Baghdad as deputy head of mission for five months before the Second Gulf War and his experience was invaluable. We saw him most days and he quickly became our closest and most trusted colleague and friend. At first, he and his staff in the British Office Baghdad worked in the grounds of the old British embassy building – I met him in the one room that was useable, with a dusty 1988 *Who's Who* and a 1989 *Wisden* on the shelf, before they set up some flat-pack offices on the cricket pitch. As the security situation got worse, they moved inside the Green Zone to a large house that had once been the home of Saddam's first wife, which acquired the nickname of 'the Bob House'.

Prince Hassan of Jordan was also very supportive. He told us that he didn't think the word 'tolerance' would do – we all need to do far more than tolerate each other, we need to respect each other. Of course, he was right and we immediately stopped talking about an Institute of Religious Tolerance and started planning an Iraqi Centre for Reconciliation and Peace.

Increasingly now we were operating from the office of the

Episcopalian chaplain to the CPA, Colonel Frank Wismer, a wise, warm-hearted man and a wonderful pastor to the strange community of thousands camped out in the Palace. Throughout this time I was assisted by the indispensable Georges Sada and another fine young man from Coventry Cathedral, Tom Kingston. (Like Oliver, Tom is a product of the public-school system with links to Holy Trinity Brompton and the Stewards' Trust – we often laugh about the fact that all the ICR's project officers belong to the same tribe. The only problem with him is his long blond hair, which makes him very conspicuous in Iraq. Once the abduction of foreigners began in 2004, we had to wrap his head in a *kafiya* whenever he left the Green Zone.)

Like everybody engaged in the reconstruction of Iraq, my colleagues worked tirelessly from early morning until late at night, with no time for rest. I was used to working all hours, but I was sometimes very worried about them: they persevered with total passion. I was reminded of an illustration I once heard about two workmen engaged in building Coventry Cathedral. When they were asked what they were doing, the first explained that he was putting lead in the window frames to hold the glass in place, but the second said he was building a cathedral. If anyone asked Georges or Tom what they were doing, they would say they were helping to rebuild a nation.

Hour after hour, day after day, we would do the rounds of the key players – religious, political and diplomatic, Iraqi, American and British. It was particularly important to establish relationships with the Sunni leaders of the nation, but our crucial contact in that community before the war, Sheikh Dr Abdel Latif Humayem, had disappeared. The 'Iraqi Billy Graham' was a delightful man, but he had been in effect Saddam's personal imam, making the pilgrimage to Mecca on the dictator's behalf and reportedly writing a copy of the Qur'an in his blood, and he had also been president of the Islamic Bank of Iraq. As a result, he was afraid to show his face in the new Iraq.

An American diplomat, Andy Morrison, another wonderful man whose department in the Palace was known as 'Baghdad Central', introduced us to Sheikh Jamal al-Badri, an important man who was responsible for organizing *Hajj* for his community, and it was he who introduced us to much of the rest of the Sunni leadership. These meetings could be very difficult. My first session with Sheikh Abdel Karda al-Ani, in a splendid house in the prosperous Baghdad neighbourhood of al-Mansur, did not start well. He was convinced that I was an agent from the CIA sent by the Americans to accuse him of being responsible for the growing insurgency. The conversation became more heated, and he chain-smoked as I tried to persuade him that all we were trying to do was to get the religious leaders to work together. It occurred to me to tell him that Sheikh Abdel Latif was my friend, and Georges then spoke up and explained that I had been working in Iraq for years and had good relationships with many prominent Sunna. Within minutes, a highly volatile encounter had turned into the beginnings of friendship. We embraced each other and finally I had his complete commitment to work with me.

All of my other meetings with Sunni leaders were as tricky to begin with, but all ended well. I remember my first visit to the Mother of All Battles Mosque, a spectacular building constructed after the Second Gulf War, with four inner minarets shaped like Scud missiles and four outer ones resembling Kalashnikovs. Here we had the first of many sessions with Sheikh Dr Harith al-Dari, the head of the Sunni Association of Muslim Scholars. He too made a commitment to work with us, but the atmosphere was not good and I realized that he was going to be very difficult.

I needed Sheikh Abdel Latif now more than ever if we were

going to make any real headway with his increasingly disenfranchised community. Eventually, with the help of Prince Raad of
Jordan and his son Prince Mired, we tracked him down in
Amman. He greeted me as warmly as ever, and told me that he
wanted to go back to Iraq but needed some assurance that he
would not be arrested. Back in Baghdad, I worked hard for his
return, and for his part he did all he could do from outside the
country to facilitate our work. He told us which Sunna we should
engage with as a matter of priority, advised us on the right
approach and prepared the ground for us before we went to see
them. After the capture of Saddam in December 2003 he became
all the more helpful, and the attitude of some of the other Sunni
leaders changed dramatically. They seemed to be resigned to the
fact that Iraq had changed for ever.

At the same time we were also engaging with Shia leaders.
Several had returned to Iraq after years in exile and among these
was Sayed Abdel Aziz al-Hakim, whose brother the ayatollah
had been assassinated in Najaf the previous year. Our meeting
with him was another bizarre experience. He was living in the
house previously owned by Tariq Aziz and I sat with him in the
very room where I had once talked with Saddam's deputy prime
minister. Little had changed in the house apart from the increased
security. We paid our condolences, asked for his support for our
endeavours and listened to his hopes for the new Iraq. At the
time, he was holding the presidency of the Governing Council, a
position that rotated every month.

Just up the road lived another prominent Shia leader, Sayed
Iyad Jamal al-Adin. He was very warm and turned out to be
strongly in favour of secular government. He had recently
returned from the UAE and like many of those who had been
living in exile he had had family killed by Saddam's regime.
Although he too was a prominent cleric, he had very little that

was positive to say about Islam over the past 500 years but instead recited a litany of the mistakes that Muslims had made, from their treatment of women to their lack of tolerance for other faiths. He was scathing about Islamic states and made it clear that his passion was to try to ensure that nothing of the kind came to birth in the new Iraq. Assisting him was somebody else who had returned from exile, in Britain: Hamid al-Sharifi, who too was in time to become a crucial ally.

Of the other ayatollahs, I had a long and very moving meeting with Hadi al-Madrasi in the holy shrine of Karbala a year after the end of the war, when he expressed his support for what we were doing. The Grand Ayatollah Ali Sistani I have never met, although he is the most authoritative figure in Iraq. He is a very holy man and a recluse and, except when he ventures abroad for medical treatment, he refuses to meet anyone who is not Iraqi. His influence in the country, both spiritual and political, is enormous, and no major decisions have been made by the Governing Council or the interim government without his support. Fortunately, he is very moderate and favours a secular democracy within certain constraints. We also know, through Ayatollah al-Sadr and Dr Mowaffak, that he strongly approves of our pursuit of dialogue and reconciliation.

Georges was still working tirelessly with us and at times he looked close to collapse, but he never gave up. One day, Frank Wismer told me that he had been asked if he knew of any Iraqi who could play a key role in the new Ministry of Defence and that Georges, with his airforce background, his reliability and his commitment to the new Iraq, was an obvious choice. I worried about how I was going to cope without him. Later that week, Fadel Alfatlawi, my friend from Coventry, came to see me to collect some things his wife had sent over with me from Britain. Fadel had fled Iraq as a teenager after the Ba'thists had killed his father and his brother, but had recently returned. It was good to talk to him, and at the end I felt it right to ask him to join our team. He had no direct experience of working for peace and reconciliation but he was very familiar with the ministry of Coventry Cathedral, ever since he translated for us when the three Iraqi religious leaders came to Britain in 1999.

Georges was at first none too pleased with this new appointment (and I admitted I was wrong not to consult him), but it was soon apparent that he was going to get a very senior position in the Ministry of Defence and he had to spend more and more time at the Palace preparing for it. Before long he was working full-time at the ministry as its most senior civil servant – and yet, despite his long hours there, he remained very involved with all we were doing. Fadel increasingly took on the role of our key man in Baghdad and I thanked God for him. He and Georges became good friends and we all worked well together.

In one of our regular meetings at the Bob House, Christopher Segar told us that we ought to meet a man called Professor Sadoon al-Zubaydi. He proved to be a kindly, sophisticated and very clever man in his late fifties who had spent many years both studying and teaching Shakespeare in Birmingham and Stratford. He too was to become a crucial part of our team. Some people treated him with suspicion, however, because he had previously been Iraq's ambassador to Indonesia and, before that, had been Saddam's chief translator and in that capacity was often seen on television. Once when he came to England he was greeted like a long-lost friend by the people at the Shakespeare Institute – but then was interrogated by my five-year-old son Jacob, who wanted to know if he was as wicked as Saddam.

Every year, on the anniversary of the bombing of the old Coventry Cathedral, a peace prize is awarded to someone who has made a significant contribution to world peace and reconciliation. The recipient is chosen early in the year, but in 2003, with all the problems in Iraq, the decision was delayed until the spring. By the time the bishop, the dean and my colleague Justin Welby came to make their decision, it was clear that there were two outstanding candidates, both Iraqis, both crucial to our work, one Shia and one Christian: Ayatollah Hussein al-Sadr and Georges Sada. They agreed to share the honour. It was the second time the Coventry International Prize for Peace and Reconciliation had been awarded for service to Iraq – the first had been in 2000, on the 60th anniversary of the bombing, when it went to Count Hans von Sponeck, the former UN humanitarian co-ordinator in Baghdad.

The date of the presentation was set, as ever, for 14 November. Even before we set off for Coventry from Baghdad, it was clear that the event was going to be much more significant than just the presentation of a prize. Two members of the Iraqi Governing Council were going to join the delegation: Mowaffak al-Rubaie and its one Christian member, Yonadam Kana. Christopher Segar thought it important that they all should come, complete with press officers and security, and said the British government would help towards the cost of bringing everyone over.

Sadly, the ayatollah was taken ill the day before the party was due to leave Baghdad, but his old friend and disciple Dr Mowaffak agreed to receive the prize on his behalf. As it turned out, it was very fortunate that members of the Governing Council were among our party, for they spent nearly a week in London before coming to Coventry in an exhaustive round of meetings at the Foreign Office and Lambeth Palace. Among others, we called on my old friend John Sawers, who was now the political director of the Foreign Office; the Archbishop of Canterbury; and the Queen's cousin Prince Michael of Kent, a strong supporter of the ICR who showed great insight into the situation in Iraq.

We also met Baroness Symons, who as Minister of State for the Middle East is very involved in our work in Israel/Palestine and as a Christian appreciates the significance of the spiritual side of the search for peace. She expressed her total support for the idea of an Iraqi Institute of Religious Tolerance, as we were then still calling it. She also stressed the need to ensure that the rights of women and children were enshrined in the new Iraq.

Immediately after the presentation we returned to the Middle East, first to Israel and then Jordan, where we called on Prince Raad. He was of course overjoyed that Saddam's evil regime had finally been overthrown, but he was deeply anxious about the future of his nation. There was at this point a growing number of people calling for the re-establishment of the monarchy, but the prince was very cautious about the idea. Although he is the rightful heir to the throne of Iraq, he was very careful to say that he was willing to do whatever he could for his people, but as for being king, only they could decide. We were to have many more meetings with him to discuss the reconstruction of Iraq and in time we became good friends. He is a wise man and our conversations with him have proved to be some of the most helpful we have had in discerning how we should proceed in the new Iraq.

We flew to Iraq the next morning. The plane was considerably bigger than the 12-seater we had flown in before and we wondered how it would manage the corkscrew landing. In fact, it did it a lot more easily. The first thing we did when we touched down was to phone home to say that we had arrived safely – and it was then that we learned, from Caroline, my wife, and from Oliver's mother, that a civilian plane had been hit by a surface-to-air missile over Baghdad International. With no more than three civilian flights into the city each day, you can imagine that our families were rather worried by this news. Once again we had escaped disaster.

Just hours before we landed in Baghdad both the Palestine and the Sheraton next door had been hit by missiles. No one had been killed but one person had been critically injured. As we drove into the city we spoke to Doug Roper, our senior administrator in Coventry, only to learn that our insurance company was no longer willing to cover us if we stayed at the Palestine. We decided to consult Christopher Segar, but he assured us that, despite the recent attacks, it was still the safest place. When we reached the hotel, we found that it was now more heavily fortified than ever. The whole neighbourhood was now completely barricaded and surrounded with tanks, razor wire and Iraqi security guards.

With us on this trip was Dr R. T. Kendall, a prominent American evangelical who for 25 years had been minister of Westminster Chapel in London. There are very few people who would embark on a trip to Israel / Palestine, Jordan and Iraq at the age of 67, and he is a courageous man. His original reason for joining us was that he wanted to visit Yasser Arafat. Having accompanied us to the Middle East 17 months earlier, he had felt compelled to return with us so that he could share the gospel with Mr Arafat and pray with him. He had had a good meeting with him the week before, and now he was coming with us on the really dangerous part of the trip.

He preached at the Palace the following morning. Saddam's throne-room was now being used as a dormitory for the CPA staff evacuated from al-Rashid after the lethal missile attacks there, and so the chapel was now set up in a tent in the palace grounds – but the grand furnishings and the throne were there. Dr Kendall spoke on 'total forgiveness' and applied the message very tellingly to the current situation in Iraq.

Our main project now was co-ordinating the establishment of the Iraqi Centre for Dialogue, Reconciliation and Peace. By January 2004, we had the draft of a ten-point document that we were going to try to get all the key religious leaders to sign. We had based it on the wording of the Alexandria Declaration of the religious leaders of the 'Holy Land', on which we had spent many months two years before. The context of that declaration was obviously very different, but we felt that it provided an appropriate model.

Each day we would spend time with the different religious groups, trying to win their approval and making amendments as necessary. With all the talk of democracy, people were clearly very anxious to ensure that the rights of their own particular community were observed and respected. It was arduous work. Often I would get back to the hotel late at night to find people waiting for me. They would tell me how important they were and then tell me how important I was, how I was the one person who could really address the needs of their community. Often they would ask me to introduce them to Paul Bremer or Sir Jeremy Greenstock. They would all say nice things about the British and insist that we understood Iraq better than the Americans. The first few times this may have been convincing, but after I had listened to it daily for several weeks its appeal began to wane.

The CPA had been anxious to acknowledge the importance especially of the Shia leaders returning from exile, and had been giving out plum positions and even the homes of senior members of the old regime. As a result, everyone was trying to prove that they were the most senior figure in their community – and their community always numbered hundreds of thousands, if not millions. Occasionally the wrong people were honoured, people who had no great influence, and this was a very real problem.

Among the Shia there was usually a sense of unity and

common purpose, not least because it is part of their culture to defer to the authority of the ayatollahs, who all consult among themselves. The Sunna do not have the same mindset and, now that we had developed good relationships with their various leaders, our next challenge was to get them to work with each other. On one occasion, the journalist Nicholas Blandford joined us for a typical meeting at the Mother of All Battles Mosque with the leaders of two Sunni organizations who could not agree on how to deal with the CPA. This is part of his account for the *Christian Science Monitor*:

> In his black suit and shirt and white collar, the tall British clergyman stands out among the gathering of Sunni Muslim clerics in flowing robes, white turbans, and colored headdresses.
>
> The Rev. Canon Andrew White nods thoughtfully as he reads a statement by one of the sheikhs criticizing the 'embarrassing failure' of the US-led Coalition Provisional Authority in Iraq and accusing the US-appointed Governing Council of being unrepresentative. The statement also condemns violence, urging instead 'constructive resistance' against the occupation, such as peaceful protests and civil disobedience.
>
> 'It's good,' says Mr White. 'I like it because I'm not an American nor a member of the Governing Council,' the Anglican minister jokes, raising a laugh from the Sunni clerics . . .
>
> White tells the assembled Sunni clerics . . . 'You will be even more powerful if the Sunnis and the Shiites can get together and take your issues to the coalition authorities together because these issues are the same.' One Sunni cleric nods his head and says, 'Negotiations are very good

and always bring about one's objectives.' It's conflict resolution at work.

The meeting breaks up earlier than expected with the two groups agreeing to present a joint front in future dealings with the CPA. White smiles broadly, pleased at the unexpectedly swift and successful outcome.

'If they had spent three days on their own, they would not have come up with that solution,' he says. 'If we can get them to come together as one group, that will be great.'

To some extent I would change my tune when I was talking to the Sunna. My close relations with the Coalition made them rather suspicious of me, so I would often emphasize the contacts I had with Iraq in the days of Saddam. The fact that I am a priest was an advantage in all my dealings with religious leaders, as they respected me as a man of God, and the fact that I am an Anglican gave me some credibility with the Sunna, who remembered that the head of my church, Dr Rowan Williams, had spoken out strongly against the war.

Our conversations with the Sunna were now taking place primarily through Da'wa al-Fatwa, a new coalition of Sunni leaders administered by Sheikh Jamal al-Badri, who was also playing a significant role in the Ministry of Religious Affairs. We met him several times and there seemed to be a real meeting of minds and a genuine commitment to the project of reconciliation.

We were also starting to engage in earnest with the Christian leadership. Raphael I Bidawid had died by now and after an interregnum of many months the Pope had finally ratified as the new patriarch Archbishop Immanuel Deli. We went to see him the day before his enthronement and took him the greetings of the Anglican Bishop, Clive Handford, who he knew. By this stage, young David was coming with us to many of our meetings.

Usually he stayed in the car but this time he wanted to come in to greet the new patriarch, and so it was that we learned that David was fluent in Aramaic.

We soon realized that Iraq's Christians were afraid of being caught in the crossfire between the Shia and the Sunna and were feeling very vulnerable. The patriarch was obviously pleased when we attended his enthronement, but he would make no promises when we asked him if he would come and sign our declaration. As for all the other Christian leaders, it was clear they were all looking to him for a lead. It was not easy for me to win over even those people who shared my own faith.

Doesn't religion do more harm than good?

It is often said that religion is the principal cause of conflict in the
world today. I am regularly invited to take part in debates on just
such a motion, which I am expected to oppose; but in fact I find
it very difficult to argue against it. Sadly religion often does play
a very negative role in world affairs – to pretend otherwise is to
close one's eyes to reality. Religion has power, and that power is
a force for evil as well as good. It is like a hammer and chisel: you
can create something beautiful with it or you can wreak total
havoc.

It is important that we do not assume that every conflict is religious in nature. Saddam Hussein was not a religious man,
though in later years he often tried to project himself as one, and
the war to oust him had no religious cause or content (though
there were some on both sides who talked about it in religious
terms). Nevertheless, religion soon did raise its head in the
conflict that ensued after the war. There is one major religious
divide in Iraq, between Shia and Sunni Muslims. This division
goes back to the early history of Islam, when a group of
Mohammed's followers saw his cousin and son-in-law Ali ibn
Abu Talib as his rightful successor, ignoring the three caliphs
before Ali who were acknowledged by the majority of Muslims.
The majority became known as Sunna, the dissidents as Shia.

As the insurgency in Iraq developed, its religious elements
became increasingly prominent. The first major sign of *intra*religious conflict was the assassination of my friend Ayatollah Abdel
Majid al-Khoi, which is commonly supposed to have been done
at the behest of a fellow Shia cleric, Muqtada al-Sadr. This was
evidently a case of internal rivalry. It was not long before there
was also fierce conflict between Shia and Sunna. For decades, the
Sunni minority in Iraq had enjoyed a near monopoly on power,

but after the war everything changed. The Shia, who had been severely persecuted under Saddam, rapidly gained the political upper hand – and the Sunna then struck back with attacks on Shia strongholds.

A more recent development has been a series of orchestrated attacks against Christians and churches in Mosul and Baghdad. Although Christianity took root in Iraq long before it became established in Europe, it has come to be identified with the West and so the invasion and occupation of Iraq is seen by many Muslims as a new Crusade designed to destroy an Islamic state. The Sunna of Falluja were all the more convinced of this when American troops launched their onslaught against the city in November 2004 on one of the holiest days of Ramadan. The date was probably chosen with no thought of its religious significance, but it had a profoundly negative effect on the local Islamic leadership. Many Christians in Iraq feel threatened by the new mood of intolerance, if not hostility, and already as many as 40,000 have left the country altogether.

We do not want to admit that religion plays a major role in conflict, but in the Middle East there is little secularism. Almost 13 years of sanctions against Iraq only served to drive people into a more extreme form of religion, a familiar phenomenon in times of suffering. Iraq had been something of a haven of tolerance for centuries but it rapidly began to fall into the malign grip of sectarianism. Religion once again had to prove its power – and sadly, as so often in difficult times, it demonstrated that power in a destructive manner. This has been aggravated by the influx from surrounding countries of various non-Iraqi radicals, both Sunni and Shia – though the more anarchic have generally been Sunni, simply because they do not have the clearly defined leadership one finds in Shia Islam.

However, if religion is the cause of much conflict, it can also be the cure to it. Even while the 'holy warriors' have been waging war in Iraq, there have been far more clerics and religious leaders calling for tolerance, respect and peace between people of different tribes and faiths. Sadly, their voices are often not heard. The signing of the Baghdad Religious Accord in February 2004 and the eventual founding of the Iraqi Institute of Peace were a declaration by the majority of Iraq's religious leaders that they would not permit intolerance and violence in the name of God to prevail. But merely to tolerate each other, they said, was not enough. What was needed was active dialogue and reconciliation. Here was a practical example of religious leaders making something lasting and lovely, using the hammer and chisel of faith to create a monument to peace.

It is a sad fact that religion is playing so big a role in the conflict in Iraq. It is only by searching for religious solutions that we will find the answer to this scourge. As much effort needs to be invested in teaching people how to create beautiful sculpture as is put into training the new security forces. Only then will Iraqi society once again be the garden of tranquillity it was meant to be.

Chapter 7

Signing up

Finally the great day arrived for the signing of the Baghdad Religious Accord. It was to be co-chaired by three members of the Iraqi Governing Council: the Shia Mowaffak al-Rubaie, the Sunni Nasir al-Chaderchi and the Christian Yonadam Kana. The venue was to be the Babylon Hotel, the biggest and safest place in Baghdad that wasn't guarded by foreigners. As we arrived on 24 February 2004 we were feeling somewhat anxious, for we did not know who would turn up. The international media were there, along with our core team of Georges, Fadel, Samir, Tom and me – but for an hour after the advertised time that was all. It's not unusual in the Middle East for people to be late, but the wait was certainly worrying.

Eventually, people started arriving – Christians, Shia and Sunna, and representatives of the smaller religious minorities, the Mandians, Yazidi and others. Many of these people had never been in the same room before, let alone sat next to each other. Among all the elaborately dressed men was a solitary woman: Mrs Samia Aziz Mohamed, the leader of the (Shia) Faili Kurds, who was to become a crucial part of our work in the months to come. Also present were several individuals who represented some of those known to be behind the insurgency. At the head of the table sat Ayatollah Hussein al-Sadr side by side with Sheikh Abdel Karda al-Ani, two of Baghdad's most eminent Muslims – who had never met each other before. The old claim that there is no difference between Shia and Sunna was clearly untrue.

Finally, the room filled up and, under the skilful chairmanship of Dr Mowaffak, the historic meeting began. The first part of the day was spent in general discussion of the need for the religious leaders to play a central role in the search for reconciliation in the new Iraq. Then we began to look at the actual declaration. Various words were debated, and in particular it was agreed that 'tolerance' was not enough – the new centre that was to pursue the aims of the accord must have 'dialogue' in its title. I and my British colleagues kept a low profile throughout to ensure that the meeting was totally Iraqi in character, though most people present knew us well. And then the meeting was over and ultimately 39 signatures were attached to the accord. There was a sense not just of relief but of triumph, though in many ways this was just the beginning of our work. For the first time in the country's history, Iraq's religious leaders had agreed to work together.

We decided that next day we would hold a dinner to celebrate at the home of Ayatollah al-Sadr, whom everyone acknowledged as the father of the accord. The meal was attended by Paul Bremer and Frank Ricciardone (America's ambassador to the Philippines, who was now co-ordinating Iraq's transition to sovereignty with the retired General Mick Kicklighter), Sir Jeremy Greenstock and Christopher Segar. The security was intense. Most of the neighbourhood was cut off by road blocks, and helicopters circled overhead, while our guests were surrounded by armed guards. Earlier that day Mr Bremer's office had called to ask if he could bring his older brother, who was on holiday paying him a visit. It was a bizarre touch of the ordinary in the heightened world in which we lived and worked. Also present were some of the Assyrian archbishops. In the end, all of Iraq's Christian clergy had stayed away from the signing because of the Chaldean patriarch's fears, but now they had heard of its success they all wanted to add their names to the accord.

Before we ate, we all sat in the 'saloon' and discussed the

1. Lost in thought outside St George's Church in Baghdad.

2. 'Playing with the Devil' – or, at least, presenting Tariq Aziz with a bottle of HP Sauce.

3. Ayatollah Hussein al-Sadr, Raphael I Bidawid (with an aide behind him) and Sheikh Dr Abdel Latif Humayem with the author in the ruins of the old Coventry Cathedral in 1999. In those days, the sheikh had both power and prestige, while the ayatollah lived in fear. After the war, their situations were very much reversed.

4. Meeting with Ayatollah al-Sadr in freedom at last.

5. The reopening of St George's in May 2003, for the first service there since 1991. Justin Welby is in the front row, in white, and to his left stand Yonadam Kana, Hanna the caretaker, Mar Addai II and Georges Sada.

6. Trying out Saddam Hussein's gold-plated throne. The mural of Scud missiles rather dominated the room, which was used first as a chapel and later as a dormitory. In the end, the throne was removed to the basement, as it was becoming too much of an attraction.

7. Walking through the gold market in Baghdad before the war.
In those days there was no need for a screen of armed guards.

8. Approaching the Palestine towards the end of 2003. By now it was more
like a prison than a hotel. The Abrams tank is blocking the road to any
would-be suicide car bombers.

9. With some of my best friends in Baghdad.

10. Looking over the Baghdad Religious Accord with
Mowaffak al-Rubaie and one of his aides.

11. In the 'saloon' of Ayatollah al-Sadr's house to celebrate the signing of the accord. Standing (left to right): Frank Ricciardone, Christopher Segar, Yonadam Kana, Nasir al-Chaderchi, Sir Jeremy Greenstock, Mowaffak al-Rubaie, Georges Sada, Avak Asadurian (the Primate of the Armenian Church in Iraq), Fadel Alfatlawi, the author and Tom Kingston. Seated (left to right): Mar Addai II, Ayatollah al-Sadr, Paul Bremer and Mar Georges Sliwa, the Archbishop of Baghdad in the Ancient Church of the East (New Calendar).

12. Yonadam Kana, the author, Iyad Allawi (then Prime Minister) and Georges Sada, shortly after the handover of sovereignty to the interim government.

previous day's business. I was reminded of the prophetic narratives of the Old Testament as the bearded ayatollah and Mr Bremer, the 'king' of Iraq, talked earnestly through an interpreter about all that had happened. The ayatollah expressed immense gratitude to America and Britain and the whole Coalition for liberating his country. He said that the sun was again shining on his nation, which had been in darkness for so long. Then he leant towards Mr Bremer and said, 'You know, this is really the work of Allah.' Mr Bremer replied: 'That is certainly what the President believes.' The conversation that followed would have boiled the blood of most Democrats. As they talked of God's interventions in history and of America's unique role as his agent, the British diplomats listening made no comment.

Then, with the helicopters clattering overhead, we went into the garden for what would conservatively be described as a 'feast'. Every Iraqi delicacy was laid before us: *masguf, biryani, qorsi,* kebabs. We talked about our plans for the Iraqi Centre for Dialogue, Reconciliation and Peace, now brought almost miraculously to birth, and ate until we could eat no more.

The ICDRP set to work the very next day trying to build religious and tribal harmony. We formed six working parties we called 'forums' to oversee the different aspects of our task:

- women, religion and democracy;
- youth and young people;
- the media;
- religious freedom and human rights;
- interreligious dialogue;
- conflict prevention and resolution.

It was a comprehensive list for a comprehensive task. From the beginning, our aim was to be as holistic in our approach as possible. From the beginning, too, it was clear that it was going to be an uphill struggle.

One major obstacle was that we still didn't have our own head-quarters – we were working between our rooms at the Palestine Hotel and the various departments at the Palace. Most of the con-fiscated Ba'th Party properties had by now been allocated and it was proving very difficult to find a building in an acceptable part of the city. After much fruitless searching and frustrating viewing, our new chair, Dr Mowaffak, suggested that we look at a house owned by his wife in the Shia neighbourhood of al-Kadamir, close to where the ayatollah lived, which he offered to us at a fraction of the going rate. Though it was not in the most neutral of locations, it was very large and beautifully situated overlooking the Tigris. We decided we had to have it, and imme-diately started work on its renovation. At the same time we were working hard to secure long-term funding. So far, most of our funds had come either from individuals overseas or from the British government via the ever supportive Christopher Segar.

We finally moved in early in June 2004 and quickly began to assemble a strong team. Now that Georges was working for the new government, Fadel took charge of things as our secretary general. Samir, who had first worked for us as my driver, was actually a lawyer and he soon assumed the role of Fadel's number two. Our head of administration was Nazera Ismail, a wonderful Faili Kurdish woman who had been chased out of Iraq by the old regime and had only just returned after many years of exile in Iran. She spoke Arabic, English and Farsi, which made her a very valuable addition to the team. She had been intro-duced to us by Mrs Samia, who was now directing our work with women. What with security people and domestic staff, there were now more than 20 of us.

Once we were settled in, we began to make arrangements for

the official opening later in the month. The fulfilment of so many hopes, this was to be a major event. Copious amounts of food were prepared for the diplomats, politicians and religious leaders who would be the guests. The evening when it came was pleasantly hot and as bright as day. As I looked out of the window, the sun was glittering on the Tigris, and on the other side of the river I could see the beautiful skyline of the Sunni neighbourhood of Adhamiya and the shimmering turquoise domes of its mosques. It could have been the most beautiful and peaceful place in the world if it had not been in the middle of a war zone.

Soon the security turned up. The road was cut off and little David once again took control of who was to be allowed through the barriers. We had really wanted to keep a low profile, but it was not to be. As the guests arrived, I stood in the garden and counted 39 guards with MP5 submachineguns surrounding the building. The speeches were short and upbeat and were delivered by Christopher Segar and Dr Mowaffak (both in Arabic) and me. After six years of struggling along the difficult road to reconciliation in Iraq, we finally had a vehicle to take us forward at speed. For me it was a highly emotional occasion.

People started visiting the centre almost immediately. Our location in a Shia neighbourhood didn't seem to deter anyone, and many of them were Sunni. Of the six forums, the women's group took the lead. They were very opposed to the law that allowed polygamy, but when this came up at the weekly meeting of the centre's executive council all the clerics spoke out against the women – until I asked them if they really wanted more than one mother-in-law. The case was not helped when the new president of Iraq took another wife, who just happened to be a minister in the interim government.

Another issue for this forum was the physical abuse of women, which is very serious in Iraq. I was shocked to hear of the scale of this problem. I decided to call in all our male staff and ask them if they beat their wives, and all except one said they did. They then started making excuses: 'What if she doesn't do what I tell her to?' I gave them strict instructions that now they were working for a centre for peace they must stop this behaviour. I was convinced that I was right to say this, but I couldn't help feeling a little anxious that I might sound like a colonial master.

Now we were a real community, living together and working all hours. The number of visitors increased each day and, despite the difficulties we faced, the centre was a very happy place. When David finally moved in with us, I think he thought he had died and gone to heaven – an enormous house with a swimming pool, wonderful gardens and his own security guards to annoy round the clock.

The centre proved to be a most wonderful place in which to work. Every day, as I sat at my desk overlooking the Tigris, I would feel overwhelmed by the glorious surroundings. But there was never any cause to be complacent. The tanks would rumble by on the road between us and the river; and from time to time we would have to run downstairs and shelter under a table when a salvo of mortar bombs came over from Adhamiya. One night at about 11 p.m. I heard David shouting for me from the garden. I ran outside to see him standing over three young lads, all much older and bigger than him. He had caught some opportunist thieves and had just copied what the American soldiers did. He got them on the ground with the aid of a baton, tied their hands behind their backs and took their ID cards. Our security guards did not treat them so kindly.

It was while I was sitting at my desk one night that I considered the centre's rather unwieldy title: 'ICDRP' was just about manageable but the unabbreviated name was not. I toyed with other possibilities and eventually came up with the 'Iraqi Institute of Peace'. The suggestion immediately gained the support of the whole executive. From then on we were known as the 'IIP', though to this day the house is referred to as the 'Centre', in both Arabic and English.

Funding was still a real problem and we spent days just writing proposals. Eventually, the Foreign Office sent out a former ambassador to Kuwait, Richard Muir, who knew the region well and had himself been responsible with us for a very significant meeting of Iraq's religious leaders that had taken place at Windsor Castle in the spring under the auspices of the Interfaith Foundation. His visit to Baghdad was very helpful. He not only wrote a positive report on our work which resulted in a very considerable injection of funds, he also gave us invaluable advice on our methods. Meanwhile, the US Institute of Peace took responsibility specifically for funding the work of the forums, while its outstanding 'head of party' in Baghdad, Heather Coyne, also provided very wise advice.

It was important for us to extend our work beyond Baghdad and so we began planning to launch the IIP in the north. We travelled to Kirkuk, Sulaymaniya and Dokan, in an area of Iraq I did not know, with beautiful rolling hills and a cooler climate. It also had much better infrastructure, as it had not been under the control of Saddam for the past 13 years. In July, in a wonderful hotel on the shores of Lake Dokan, we met with a broad spectrum of people who had gathered from the country's three northern, Kurdish governorates. The mood was very positive, though there proved to be one big problem with the accord, which we had hoped that everyone would sign. The Yazidi, a substantial minority in the north whose religion is derived from Zoroastrianism, objected to the statement that the insurgency was the work of the Devil. Yazidi believe that God is kind and the Devil is not and that therefore you have to be polite to the Devil so that he won't be angry with you. We reached a compromise, the Dokan Accord was signed and everyone undertook to set up a northern branch of the IIP based in Kirkuk.

By September, our work had grown both more extensive and more intense. The Iraqi Institute of Peace was now well respected both by the interim government and the Coalition and by the ordinary people in the neighbourhood. We were not surprised therefore when some former prisoners of the old regime came to us one fine day to ask for our help. They thought they had discovered Izzat Ibrahim al-Duri, the erstwhile vice-chair of Saddam's Revolution Command Council who was one of the few of the '55 most wanted' still at large. They knew we were in daily contact with the Coalition and the interim government and they wanted us to turn him in.

Fadel agreed to this and within minutes the suspect was eating lunch in our house. I got out my pack of cards and looked at al-Duri. There was certainly a resemblance, but I was not at all sure it was him. I spoke to my contacts in the American embassy and they assured me that the army would come and collect him. I also rang the Prime Minister's office just to let them know what was happening. After three hours and several more calls, four men of the American special forces turned up, in plain clothes and two ordinary cars, having got lost on the way. The suspect (who had remained calm and co-operative throughout) was respectfully searched and quietly taken away.

Relieved to be rid of him, we returned to our work. We were startled when, 45 minutes later, one of our guards rushed in and bundled us all up onto the roof. Nazera was pushed under a sheet of metal. We had no idea what was happening. I looked over the edge of the roof and saw that the house was surrounded by over 100 plain-clothes policemen. The road was blocked off by marked vehicles – the only indication that this was an official raid. Our guards were all lying flat on their faces. By this stage I was getting very angry. I shouted down to the men below to ask what was going on. The only response came when some of the police suddenly appeared on the roof and threatened to shoot me. When little David jumped in front of me to protect me, they hit him so hard with their guns that he fell unconscious. They then beat me.

After a little while, they went back down to the street. My main concern was for David. We carried him downstairs and placed him on a bed. It was another ten minutes before he regained consciousness. Eventually, a smartly dressed man arrived at the house and sat down in our 'saloon', as cool as you please. He turned out to be the director-general of the Ministry of Interior, but I asked our guards to remove him nonetheless. We had been given an explanation – they had come to collect the suspect, even though I had phoned the Prime Minister's office as soon as the Americans had been – but there was still no hint of an apology.

As the police began to leave, we inspected the damage. Several doors had been smashed down, locked cupboards had been broken into and over $20,000 in cash and equipment had been taken. We were severely shaken: we had been attacked and our centre had been ransacked, and it was all the work of the Iraqi government. We rang the American embassy – and within minutes a tank, an armoured personnel carrier and a Humvee were parked outside the house. It was not at all what we had wanted. We had aimed to keep our profile low but now our cover was blown and it was obvious that we would no longer be able to function as we had before. On the television it was being announced that Izzat Ibrahim al-Duri had been captured, but it soon transpired that it wasn't him at all but a relative of his, also wanted but not nearly so much.

The following day I was told by the American and British

authorities that we had to move into the Green Zone. Soon we were ensconced in a new home we were to share with the United States Institute of Peace, whose 'head of party', Heather Coyne, was already a friend and colleague. We met with various people from the Ministry of Interior, but they all but denied that the raid could have been their work and there was still no apology. On the other hand, the support we received from the British embassy was fantastic, and questions were even asked in Parliament about the incident. Baroness Symons, who had become a real friend, assured the House of Lords that I was safe and that the government had demanded an explanation.

In retrospect, the most worrying thing about this incident was the fact that the Iraqi security forces could not really be trusted. Many of the men in the new services had previously worked for Saddam, some even as killers and torturers, and they were evidently finding it hard to forget their old habits. Even more disturbing, however, was growing evidence of collusion between the security forces and some of the insurgents. Almost no one was beyond suspicion.

By now, we were also spending more and more time trying to track down hostages, as increasing numbers of people were being abducted. Each day in Baghdad, before I left the car, my driver and my guards would insist I said a prayer, and if I didn't call on God to send his angels to watch over us they would shout at me, 'Angels! Angels!' However well we were guarded by our security men, I was reminded that we relied on the protection of the angelic hosts. The situation grew ever more dangerous, and yet we had to persist with the search for peace. The task we were engaged in was unique, and we believed that our mandate was divine. The commitment that was shared by the whole team, both in Iraq and in Britain, was greater than ever. We could not give up on the Iraqi people. If they could persevere, so must we.

Can there be peace between religions?

Many people regard 'interfaith relations' as a woolly liberal Western idea, and some even question whether any such thing is appropriate in the Middle East. But contact between the leaders of different religions and sects in Baghdad is a very different matter from sitting down with cups of tea and smoked salmon bagels in London. In Iraq, where politics and religion are inextricably linked, it is often a matter of life and death. In Iraq, it is seen not as the province of liberals – there are very few such people there – but of radicals who perceive that there can be (in the famous words of Hans Küng) 'no peace among the nations without peace among the religions'.

There were encounters between the various religious groups under the Ba'thists, but usually they were not spontaneous but were instigated by the regime to try to prove a point to the outside world. This was the case when Saddam appointed the team to come to America and Britain with us in 1999. The sad reality is that the signing of the Baghdad Religious Accord in February 2004 was the first time that many of Iraq's senior religious leaders had met each other. Of particular significance was the meeting of the Shia and Sunni leadership. Obviously they knew of each other, but they had been afraid to meet before. Many still are afraid to meet, for interreligious activity in Iraq is a dangerous exercise. Some of those who have taken the risk and become involved in this new *rapprochement* have been called 'traitors' and 'collaborators'. Some have even had their property attacked.

Interfaith tolerance is not enough in itself. What we are engaged in is designed to move beyond mere tolerance to dialogue, respect and reconciliation. So often in the past in Iraq you would hear from religious and tribal leaders the party line dictated by the regime: 'We are all the same!' None of them could admit the very real divisions between the different communities. The kind of inter-religious activity we are involved in now is not an attempt to reduce the various faith traditions to the lowest common denominator. Its concern is not to gloss over even the most problematic differences but to acknowledge them. It is especially important that we understand and engage with each other's developed oral tradition. When we read each other's sacred scriptures we find in them both things that attract and things that repel us, but we all accept that these are immutable. On the other hand, the *traditions* of all our religions, even if written down, are open to change.

It was the American poet Longfellow who said, 'If we could read the secret history of our enemies, we should find in each man's life sorrow and suffering enough to disarm all hostility.' So much of what we are doing is concerned simply to enable each side to hear the story of the other. As we work to bring this about, we can see clearly that each side has suffered, each believes it is a minority and each feels it is vulnerable.

In no way are we trying to say that all religions are the same or even that they all lead to salvation. The very idea of trying to create one world religion is total anathema to everyone involved. Our objectives are, first, that the different religious communities should have enough respect for each other to stop the intercommunal killing that is often justified in the name of God and, second, that they should then embark on a journey together in search of reconciliation. For a Christian this call is Cross-centred, for we see the death of Jesus as the ultimate act of reconciliation to restore peace between humankind and God.

We also have to recognize that this kind of work must not be limited to the moderates. If it is really to bear fruit, it must include those who are generally regarded as the greatest exponents of violence. On the whole, 'nice' people do not cause wars, and so if interreligious activity involves only nice people talking to nice people it will be futile. In Iraq, there is a particularly difficult problem, which is how we should deal with those we regard as terrorists. Clearly, it is problematic for the Coalition forces to be seen to be engaging with such people. Thus, we have to assess which individuals and groups we can talk to and which need to be dealt with militarily.

In our work in Israel/Palestine we have shown that it is possible to move beyond incitement to hatred and violence to mutual respect and even love between enemies. One man who has experienced such a change is Sheikh Tal el-Sider, one of the founders of Hamas, who has totally renounced all forms of violence and accepted without reservation the path of peace and reconciliation. He has suffered greatly for this, but today he counts among his closest friends senior Israeli rabbis who are also walking this difficult road.

There is no miracle cure in this search for peace, but it is clear that *rapprochement* between different religious communities is more important than ever. Not least, this is because the West has fundamentally misunderstood Islam. The growing rift between the Muslim and the Western worlds is perhaps the biggest threat to global security today. The so-called 'war on terror' is widely interpreted as a showdown between the Islamic and Christian civilizations characterized by the American writer Benjamin Barber as Jihad versus 'MacWorld'. The invasion of Iraq has been seen by many in similar terms.

Jesus' injunction to love our enemies has never been more important. This always involves risk, but in this case it may well lead us into a complex engagement between different religious communities that in time could save the world. As the president of the International Center for Religion and Diplomacy, Douglas Johnston, has said, religion is 'the missing dimension of statecraft'.

Chapter 8

Striving to set the captives free

Hostage negotiations are not a precise science. They involve a complex, day-and-night engagement with a whole range of good and bad people. At the IIP, we talk not only to various religious and tribal leaders but also to former members of the Mukhabarat. These individuals are often our best sources of information, though we are never quite sure of their character. Some of them are clearly malignant, but others seem somewhat more benign.

The first thing one needs to establish in any such dealings is whether the victim was taken for financial or political reasons. Most of the kidnappers are small-time bandits trying to make some quick money, but if they capture a foreigner they will often sell them on to terrorists who will use them for political gain. The value of a hostage depends on his or her nationality. The British and Americans are invariably sold on to terrorists and they fetch the highest prices. Citizens of lesser members of the Coalition come cheaper. The vast majority of hostages are middle-class Iraqis or their children, who sell for very much less (and are largely ignored by the international media).

The first few days after an abduction are vital. The longer the negotiations continue, the less likelihood there is of a good outcome. People taken by Shia groups are far more easily recovered than those taken by radical Sunna. In the Shia community, there is always respect for the ayatollah and other sayeds, whereas Sunni leaders wield much less influence outside their immediate circles. Whenever a hostage is sold up the chain to Salafi, Wahhabi or al-Qa'ida-type groups, the prospects of their release become very remote – and yet every effort must still be made until there is some resolution either way.

It is essential to know who you are dealing with. In the early days, many religious and tribal leaders came forward and assured us that they were the ones who could pull the right strings. Most of them seriously exaggerated their own influence, either to increase their status in the new Iraq or because they really wanted payment. In time, we learned who could actually help us and who was just wasting our time. At first we didn't pay anyone – at most a mobile phone or a PlayStation 2 was enough to get their co-operation – but as time went by they began to demand considerable sums of money in exchange for the information they had to give us. Often they told us they had to pay the local people who had supplied it to them, but it was hard to tell if this was true. In any case, it was very difficult for us to find this sort of money, as we had no specific funds available for this work.

Should one ever actually pay a ransom? The problem is that to do so (as the Italian government is believed to have done on several occasions), or to give in to other demands (as the Philippines among others has done), only encourages the taking of yet more hostages. The easy answer is clearly 'No' – but it is rarely so black-and-white. Several prominent church leaders have been taken and their kidnappers have always demanded hundreds of thousands of dollars. Often the heads of their denominations have contacted me to ask what they should do. All I can do is tell them the truth, that they have a choice: either they pay something and their colleague will live or they pay nothing and their colleague will be killed. Whenever they have asked me how much they should pay, I have quoted a figure far lower than the sum demanded. They have always paid up and got their colleagues back alive.

These cases put me in an ethical dilemma. I am opposed to giving in to the demands of blackmailers or terrorists, but how do you put a value on the life of a friend? However, when it comes to the really serious players, such as Abu Musab al-Zarqawi's group al-Tawhid wa'al-Jihad, money is never the issue – they have plenty of it. What they want is to manipulate the political situation. It is always wrong to give in to such people.

I was checking in for the flight home from Baghdad in January 2004 when I was approached by a young man. 'You must be Father Andrew,' he said. This is the title I am known by in Israel/Palestine, so I was taken aback to hear it used in Iraq, where I am usually referred to by the locals as either '*Abuna*' or 'Brother Andrew'. It turned out that the young man was Nabil Rassouk, who was indeed from Jerusalem. I knew his family well and his first cousin Nisreen is my secretary there. I was rather surprised that no one had told me he was in Iraq, though I often sat with his father and his uncles at their shop in Jaffa Gate in the Old City of Jerusalem. (We often discussed Iraq, and in particular some very poor relatives of theirs who lived in Baghdad. They would regularly give me money to take to one of these, Vivien, who was a member of the congregation of St George's.)

It turned out that Nabil had lived and studied in America for some years and was now working in Baghdad with Research Triangle International (RTI), an American company that had been brought in by USAID to improve local governance. We talked for some time and agreed to meet up when we both returned to Iraq.

A few weeks later, on 5 April, I received a phone call from Hanna Ishaq, the ICR's local liaison officer in Jerusalem, who was also related to Nabil by marriage. He had bad news for me: Nabil had been working in Najaf and had been kidnapped by an unknown group. The family was asking me for help. It was Thursday of Holy Week and I had just returned to Britain for

Easter. Some rather frantic research established that Nabil had been shown on Arab television with another hostage and was being accused of being an Israeli and American spy. The situation was very serious. It was clear that we needed to act fast if we were to have any hope of securing his release.

I immediately drew up a ten-point action plan involving our staff in Israel/Palestine, Iraq and Britain. If we were to save Nabil, we first had to convince his kidnappers that he was not an Israeli. Over many years working in the Middle East I had forged very good relationships with both Israelis and Palestinians, and not least with Yasser Arafat and with Emil Jarjoui, a Christian member of the PLO executive. I rang Dr Jarjoui without delay to see if he could organize a letter from Mr Arafat stating that the two hostages were Palestinians and not Israelis. Within minutes I was talking to Mr Arafat himself, and within an hour I had the letter.

We soon discovered, however, that our information was wrong: the second hostage had been given the wrong name and was actually Fadi Fadel, a Canadian citizen of Syrian origin. This meant that the letter from Mr Arafat was of no use, as it identified both hostages as Palestinian. I spoke to Mr Arafat again and told him of the problem. Again within an hour a new letter had been e-mailed to us. Meanwhile, three members of our Iraqi team – Georges, Fadel and Sadoon – were working around the clock to try to ascertain who it was that was actually holding Nabil.

I had to go to America at this point and so I was on a different time from my colleagues in Iraq and the family in Israel. For several days, I spent most of the night on the phone to Baghdad and Jerusalem. Then on day ten we learned that Fadi had been released and were assured by various sources that Nabil too had been freed. Several hours passed and we heard nothing more. We were becoming very concerned, but the agony for Nabil's family must have been unbearable. The following day, Georges made contact with the chief of police in Najaf, who told him that Nabil was not with them. We soon realized that the reports of his release had been wrong. The negotiations began again with even greater intensity. RTI had brought in a hostage-release company called the Ackerman Group and we kept in constant touch with their staff, though we don't know the nature of their negotiations. We also talked regularly to the CPA.

We had to make use of all our contacts in Iraq – as we put it, with the bad guys as well as the good ones. One of our most eminent Shia friends spoke to the renegade young cleric Muqtada al-Sadr, who informed us that his militia did not have Nabil but confirmed that he was probably in or near Najaf. Finally, Fadel called on the services of some members of the Islamic Da'wa Party whom he knew. They thought they knew where Nabil was and agreed to go to Najaf to find him. That night, they rang us to say that he was safe and would be released the next day. By this stage, however, I did not believe any promises.

In fact, we worked on Nabil's case day and night for another week. He was finally freed on 22 April. We don't know whose efforts it was in the end that secured his release. When I met up with him a few days later at his family's home on the outskirts of Jerusalem, he was obviously traumatized by his experience. His family were grateful for all we had done and presented me with a beautiful icon painted on an ostrich egg.

If those negotiations had been intensive and exhausting, they were nothing compared with what was to come. In reality, Nabil was one of the lucky ones: other hostages were held for many more weeks, and many did not survive. We soon started working on many of the other cases. We spent a lot of time in April and May working with the Italian ambassador on the case of three of his countrymen who were held – a fourth had already been killed on camera.

The spate of abductions continued unabated after the handover of sovereignty in June 2004 and in fact has now become so severe that we can only get involved where the government of a particular hostage asks for our help. An increasing number of truck drivers from the developing world have been taken and many have been brutally murdered, often on camera. Others are simply never heard of again. We organized a joint *fatwa* (a ruling on a point of religious law) from Sunni and Shia clerics that condemned both insurgency and the taking of hostages, but it did little good – the kidnappers have scant respect for the Islamic authorities.

Often the negotiations involve meetings late at night in odd and even dangerous locations, but when I advise my colleagues against going at such times to such places, and usually they just respond, 'But, *Abuna*, we have to try and save them.' Peculiar-looking men will turn up at the Centre, often also at strange times, and give us detailed information about what is going on in their neighbourhoods. Often it is the women on our team who prove to be the most useful. They will go into the thick of a conflict zone to meet the people who really do have influence. However, many of the key leaders in the Sunni areas have fled in fear for their own lives, and often we have to meet these people in neighbouring countries.

We now have members of our conflict-resolution team 'embedded' in some of the most dangerous parts of the country. Every day they are working to get the local religious and tribal leaders to engage with each other, and every day they keep us informed about what is going on – or what will happen if nothing is done to prevent it. Often the issues are things we can do nothing about, though sometimes we can discuss them with the interim government or the US Army. Very often people will say they will deal with me simply because I am from the Anglican church, one of the few organizations trusted by the Sunna because of our work in Iraq before the war.

It soon became clear that the British embassy was very worried about this side of our work, but when Britons were taken they asked for our help. The first high-profile case was that of the contractor Kenneth Bigley. We knew that there was very little chance of getting him released, because it was evident from the beginning that he was in the hands of al-Zarqawi, but we did not give up trying until the very bitter end.

The case of Margaret Hassan was quite different. Margaret was a friend whom I had known and admired since my first visit to Baghdad. As the Iraq director of the major relief agency Care International, she was totally dedicated to the welfare of Iraqi people. What is more, she was married to an Iraqi and had lived in the country for 30 years and held Iraqi nationality. Dealing with her case was highly stressful and very emotional. For one thing, it wasn't clear who her abductors were. They appeared to be an unknown Sunni group with no obvious religious commitment. Even al-Zarqawi apparently urged her captors to let her go.

We were making very little headway and so we decided that I should go to Jordan and the UAE to try to get a *fatwa* from Iraq's two most respected Sunna. In Amman, I went to see my old friend Sheikh Abdel Latif, with whom we had been in regular contact ever since we tracked him down there. The Care team came to the hotel and filmed his call for her release. He had himself met Margaret with me some years before and his appeal was sincere and eloquent.

I then set off for Dubai to see Sheikh Ahmed al-Qabasi, an even more senior man. He had fled Iraq some years before after falling out with Saddam, but he still exerted considerable influence through his weekly televised sermons. But even as my plane landed I received a phone call from the BBC, wanting my reaction to Margaret's execution. I really had believed there was a chance that we could secure her release, but we had failed. I rang our team in Baghdad and shared their disbelief, their horror and their silence. They too had tried so hard. Some of them refused point-blank to believe the news. On other occasions, after equally arduous attempts, we had succeeded. It was devastating.

I phoned the British consulate in Dubai and we decided at least to try to get al-Qabasi to condemn the practice of abduction. I had a good relationship with him following a previous visit, but the meeting was not as positive as I had hoped. He told me that he knew who was doing the kidnapping: it was the Americans. This made a change from Mossad, who were usually blamed, but it was still very disturbing and frustrating. That evening when I met with Anthony Harris, a member of our council and a former British ambassador to the UAE, his verdict was simple: 'Some of our friends do have a serious problem with the truth.' We had pleaded with the sheikh to speak out against kidnapping in his televised sermon the next day and he had agreed to, but what he said in the end was veiled and not as strong as we would have liked.

At the time of writing, more than 200 foreign nationals have been abducted, and many hundreds of Iraqis. Some, such as the Canadian Mohammed Rifat, have been missing since as long ago as April 2004, and there is still no word of the whereabouts of many. The anguish for their families is unbearable. We have worked on many cases and to date we have contributed directly to the release of just a dozen or so of these. Nevertheless, our efforts must continue. It isn't possible to go into details about what exactly we do, but I can say that all our friends are working with us and helping us in this endeavour. As Christians, we see this as part of the incarnational ministry that we are called to as we strive to 'set the captives free'. The many Muslims we work with are equally committed to work for mercy, justice and freedom in the spirit of the Prophet. This is the cutting edge of interfaith relations.

In February 2005, a young man in our team was brutally killed while looking for a foreign hostage. It was another shattering reminder of the dangers we face.

Where is God in all this?

Many claims are made about the role of God in human affairs, and many have been made about his role in the Third Gulf War and all that followed. Some people see God's hand in the swiftness of the initial military victory. Some people ignore the pain and chaos of recent months, focusing only on the positive and possibly glorious.

My understanding is that God is always engaged in every aspect of life. My God is the God who reveals himself in both the triumphs and the traumas of the people and the land of Iraq. Over the years that I have been involved with this nation I have seen him at work in the good times and the bad. I have seen him in the splendour of our religious services in Saddam's former throne-room in the presidential Palace in Baghdad and I have seen him in the radiance in the faces of the destitute children on the streets of that once great city. And I have seen him in extraordinary answers to prayer for people's needs.

There have been times when I have questioned God. Why is it that I have been miraculously saved from death on so many occasions but my friends have not been? Why have others who were no less God's servants been gunned down or kidnapped and brutally murdered? I continue to ask these things, but I have no answers. Yet I know that, except for Israel/Palestine, there is no land where the Bible locates so many acts of God. It was in what is now Iraq that Ezekiel saw God's glory as an exile. It was here that Daniel was rescued from the mouths of the lions. It was here that Jonah reluctantly preached to the people of Nineveh. It was here that the writer of Psalm 137 wept by the rivers of Babylon as he remembered Zion.

It was here that he asked: 'How can we sing the songs of the LORD while in a foreign land?' And that is the question I have asked more than any other over my years of involvement in Iraq. It is the question I continued to ask as the situation deteriorated so badly that at one point the Foreign Office sent me home. Back in Britain, I asked this question even more earnestly as I received daily reports of Iraq's spiral down into chaos and despair. When I am in the land of the Tigris and the Euphrates, 'the rivers of Babylon', it has been at St George's that I have gained new hope and courage. Just seeing the faces of the worshippers has been enough to spur me on in what must be one of the most challenging jobs in the world: trying to find peace in Babylon.

I am essentially a person of simple faith. I have a childlike trust in God that accepts that there is much I do not understand. I am often surprised when prayers are answered, even though I expect an answer. I do not believe that our lives are charmed, or that 'everything is going to be all right' – and yet it is a fact that week by week we have experienced extraordinary escapes from death. I would guess that there have been 17 or 18 occasions when a bomb has just missed us, sometimes by seconds.

Not that the goodness of God is reserved for Christians. Once I was asked by Ayatollah al-Sadr if I could supply meat for the Muslim festival of Eid al-Fitr. Our funds were very limited, but that night I prayed that somehow we would be able to help. The next morning I was approached at breakfast by a man I had never met before, who asked me rather abruptly if I wanted some meat. He explained that he had a shipment for the US Army that was too close to its eat-by date for their use. There were thousands of tons of best-quality meat that, as it happened, was *halal*. He even had a fleet of 43 refrigerated lorries to deliver it.

It was the most remarkable answer to prayer I have ever had. There were Christians who could not believe that 'their' God would provide for Muslims, but the God I know cares for all people, whatever their creed or race. I have seen him at work in the imam, the priest and the soldier. This doesn't mean I think that all have equal status, or that all faiths are equally valid; but it does mean I believe that God is bigger than the boxes and boundaries we put him in.

There are still many questions unanswered, and daily we ask, 'Why does the God of love allow such evil?' Yet I need only think of the times that I have witnessed God's glory and goodness in Iraq to convince me beyond doubt that he is as active in that country as he is anywhere in the world. Amidst the success and the failure, the living and the dying, we have a God who is stronger than the anarchy that grips this ruined land. It is this God who gives us the assurance that, despite the present chaos, there is at long last hope of a new Iraq where there will be true democracy, peace and respect for the other.

Chapter 9

The corridors of power

Before the war, my contacts with government in both Britain and America had been strange, to say the least. My work in Iraq had been frowned on – why was this reckless, maverick clergyman going to play with the Devil? That was the general attitude. Even Tim Sebastian, the presenter of BBC World's *Hardtalk* programme, went for me for not just going to see 'these evil bloodsuckers' but actually taking them presents. (The news had got out that I used to take HP Sauce to Tariq Aziz. It was the only thing he wanted from England – and if you are playing with the Devil, one thing you don't want to do is annoy him.)

The invitations to enter the corridors of power in London and Washington came because I had some knowledge of what was going on 'on the ground'. In the early days I was very concerned by the ignorance I encountered in both governments. The information they had about Iraq was often out of date and frequently had been given to them by the leaders of the opposition movements. And however sincere *they* were, they all had one aim in mind: the overthrow of Saddam Hussein. About this they were passionate, and this probably accounts for some of the misleading intelligence they provided.

I tried to restrict the information I passed on to matters of religion and tribalism, which were the areas I knew most about – though even here my knowledge was limited, because my contacts were afraid to speak openly. I was horrified at how little understanding there was of these particular issues in government circles. I constantly stressed that any post-war conflict was likely to be substantially religious or tribal in character, but I got the impression that they were thinking, 'Well, he would say that, wouldn't he? He's a cleric himself.' Nonetheless, there were others who were very concerned about these things in both London and Washington.

I spent many hours in America going back and forth between the National Security Council and the State Department, as well as other bodies that were being prepared to play a leading role in the reconstruction of Iraq. I recall one especially disturbing meeting when someone outlined their plan for a new ministry of religious affairs. The idea was to have a council of 12 people which would consist of six men and six women – and no clerics. This might have worked in the District of Columbia but in Iraq it would have been a disaster. Fortunately, this scheme was never pursued. Instead, unfortunately, almost nothing was done on this most important of issues. I still reflect on the dismissive letter I received from the British Foreign Office in January 2003 that told me that now was not the time to deal with religious matters.

I can remember when the truth first dawned on the British contingent in the CPA and we spent hours trawling around Saddam's old palace trying to find someone who was dealing with these issues. Certainly there were people who were interested in this side of things, but many of them seemed powerless to make anything happen. Among the exceptions were some people who were part of the Sunday morning congregation in the chapel. One such was Dayton Maxwell, a long-time employee of USAID, who took ownership of what we were trying to do and went to great lengths to ensure that we got to the right people. Throughout, we had a good relationship with both Paul Bremer and the head of the British team – first Sir Jeremy Greenstock and then David Richmond. My name was added to the short list of those who were allowed to enter 'the front office' at the Palace, where the chiefs presided.

Mr Bremer, who is known to his friends as 'Jerry', proved to be a very affable man. I got on very well with him. He seemed to enjoy his position as the 'king' of Iraq, but it was clear that he cared deeply about the Iraqi people. Sir Jeremy was an archetypal English gentleman-diplomat. Sometimes he would get frustrated when some of the American staff at the CPA did not take our work seriously, but he was always the model of tact. We found him also very approachable – and it helped to break the ice when we discovered that Oliver's housemaster at Harrow was his brother.

Within the CPA, the British were treated with respect, but sometimes there was a feeling that they would be consulted and then totally disregarded, and to some crucial meetings they were not even invited. They would often observe sanguinely, 'We mustn't forget that we're only supplying seven per cent of the troops' – but certainly there were times when they wished they had more than seven per cent of the say.

It was the Pentagon that was the source of all power. Our contacts with the American military were few in the early days, and then one lunchtime everything changed. Collecting my plastic knife and fork in the palace dining-room, I had hoped to sit with some of the British diplomats, but by the time I reached their table all the places had gone. I went and sat at the first table I could find with an empty seat and there I got talking to four older men. They seemed very interested in the nature of my work. After ten minutes or so, I asked them what their particular assignment was and they told me they had been sent by Donald Rumsfeld, the US Secretary of Defense, to assess how things were going and identify what needed to change. One of their big concerns was what was happening on the religious front. They saw our meeting as being, quite literally, providential.

Tom, Fadel and I spent much of that afternoon discussing with these delegates the challenges and difficulties presented by growing religious intolerance. We told them that the insurgency was going to spread dramatically. The Coalition had failed to keep the Sunni groups onside and they were feeling increasingly disenfranchised, and foreign extremists were exploiting this. We explained the need to allow some of the most senior Sunni leaders back into the country even if they had been close to the old regime. In particular, it was obvious that we were not going to make much headway until Sheikh Abdel Latif returned. By now we had discovered where he was, but he refused to come back until he had a guarantee from the Americans that he would not be put in prison. The problem was that neither the CIA nor the FBI wanted him in Iraq.

The response of the delegates was very positive and we promised to go and see them when we next went to Washington in a few weeks' time. One of the four, with whom we formed a particularly close relationship, was Jerry Jones, a distinguished-looking man in his sixties who worked in the Office of White House Liaison at the Pentagon. He got to work immediately on the matter of Sheikh Abdel Latif.

The principal purpose of this visit to Washington was to attend the Presidential Prayer Breakfast, an annual three-day gathering of political and religious leaders that brings together several thousand people from all over the world. We did the usual rounds of the capital and finally ended up at the Pentagon for a very encouraging meeting with Jerry. We also met David Patterson, chief of staff to Paul Wolfowitz. Jerry and David soon became our principal channels of communication with the Pentagon. Over the months that followed, there was a huge number of issues on which we needed its help and they were always forthcoming.

Another key figure with whom we still deal is Mick Kick-lighter, a retired three-star general who, with Frank Ricciardone, ran the office at the CPA that oversaw Iraq's transition to sovereignty. General Kicklighter and his assistant were regular members of our Sunday morning congregation in the Palace – they were not just churchgoers but totally committed Christians whose faith influenced every aspect of their work. For them, as for many of the staff in the Palace, 'this Iraq business' was the work of God and they were not ashamed to say so.

It very soon became clear to me that America is not the secular state it so often claims to be. In spite of its official separation of church and state, Americans proved to be very prone to seeing God at work in human affairs, and indeed at times they would discuss things of huge political significance in profoundly spiritual terms. On one occasion I was explaining to a very senior man at the Pentagon that the Foreign Office was afraid for my life and he told me emphatically, 'Andrew, nothing is going to happen to you.' When I asked him how he could be so sure, I was startled when he said: 'God told me.' This mentality is quite alien to the British, and in dealing with the two senior Coalition partners we adopted very different approaches. (In Baghdad, Frank Wismer even nominated one Sunday as 'Bring a Brit to Church Sunday'. There were many British people in the Green Zone but, unlike the Americans, very few went to church.)

However, the truth is that, once it became clear that religion was one of the principal factors in the spread of the insurgency, both the Americans and the British gave us total support. I have been careful in this book not to talk of 'Islamic extremism', because the term is so offensive to Muslims, but in reality all religions are prey to extremism, and when religion goes wrong it goes very wrong. Governments are increasingly aware that a lot of violence is rooted in religion, but they don't know how to deal with this. Faith can be the cure of conflict as much as the cause of it, but to achieve this, religious peacemakers must work closely and effectively with the secular authorities. Christopher Segar in particular understood this well. So too did many members of Iraq's interim government. In the early days of his prime ministership I would regularly go and see Iyad Allawi. Although his outlook was secular, he was intensely worried about the growing religious intolerance and he agreed to become the patron of the IIP. On one occasion we took the whole of our executive council to see him – a major undertaking, since getting in to see members of the government was even more of an ordeal than getting into the Palace.

By this stage, I had a Department of Defense pass, an American embassy pass and a British embassy pass and between them these were enough to get me in to most places. For others in our team it was harder, and at times this was embarrassing. Many of them were Iraqis of high standing after all – Christian archbishops, senior Shia and Sunni sheikhs and leading politicians – whereas I am just a visitor to their country. The entrance procedure was exhaustive, and the extreme heat made it even worse. In temperatures of 50°C, people would have to wait in line to be sniffed by dogs and searched by Gurkhas before they were finally allowed through the first gate. One might then be searched again by American soldiers before one was eventually permitted to enter the Prime Minister's office. However, by this point Georges Sada was working as Dr Allawi's chief spokesman and this was a big advantage. It gave us a degree of access that even senior government officials did not have.

Eventually, with the help of Jerry Jones and David Patterson, Sheikh Abdel Latif was given the guarantee he wanted and thousands turned out to greet him in his home town of Ramadi. He told me he had had several interviews with the CIA in Jordan. When I asked him what they wanted to know, the answer was predictable: 'What I said in the mosque on the Friday before the fall of Baghdad.' And what had he said? With his usual mischievous grin, he replied: 'I preached against America.'

Soon after his return, the sheikh asked for a meeting with the CPA, which we arranged with David Richmond (now Britain's senior diplomat in Iraq) and Richard Jones, the former American ambassador to Kuwait who was now Paul Bremer's number two. The other leading Sunni sheikhs came with him and the encounter was polite and constructive but frank. They presented a list of military and political issues that needed to be dealt with – the presence of American troops in Ramadi, the lack of respect they received and so on – and departed happy, knowing that they had been heard. As we walked through the Palace, Sheikh Abdel Latif gave us a very different tour of the building he knew so well. He showed us where Saddam would eat, where he would sit, where he would welcome guests, even where he would sleep. Some of the American staff were fascinated to learn the history of their place of work.

The following day, the news was less good. One of the sheikhs, Abdel Karda al-Ani, had been targeted by insurgents. Part of his house was blown up and a letter was left that called him a traitor and a collaborator. This was the sheikh with whom, many months before, I had had such a difficult first meeting – and now he was considered too friendly to the West. He fled Baghdad and to this day I have not seen him again. Things also started going badly for Sheikh Abdel Latif. We had barely finished celebrating his return when the National De-Ba'thification Committee decided to seize all his assets, amounting to $70 million. (The committee was chaired by Ahmed Chalabi, who was not exactly beyond reproach himself.) Neither we nor the Americans were in a position to remedy this and, no longer able to afford the security he needed, he went back to Jordan.

Although we had once been criticized by the British and

vigorously to portray the views of differing communities and interest groups. Increasingly, one has to distinguish between the Sunna, the Shia, the Christians and those from different ethnic and tribal groups, as well as between the various components of the Coalition. Iraq today is a highly complex and cosmopolitan society. The media need to understand it thoroughly if they want to make a positive contribution to its restoration.

Chapter 10

Changing regimes

Early in December 2003 I left Baghdad to travel to America, to spend some time at the inspirational All Nations Church in Charlotte, North Carolina. Over the years I have grown to love these people like my own family, and I and my family receive so much love from them in return. They have truly become my greatest source of moral and spiritual support.

It was while I was there, at about two in the morning, that I learned that Saddam had been captured. First the BBC rang me for a reaction, and minutes later I was called by people in Baghdad who filled in all the details. The rest of the night was spent giving phone interviews to the media. There was by now much jubilation on the streets of Baghdad, and when I spoke to my colleagues I could hear the sound of celebratory gunfire in the background. Then came the historic press conference where Paul Bremer announced, 'Ladies and gentlemen, we got him.' And then came the pictures – pathetic pictures of this rat-like creature found in a hole in the ground. As I saw these images, I experienced not elation but profound sorrow for all that Iraq had suffered. To my surprise, I wept as I hadn't wept since my childhood. Many of the Iraqi friends I spoke to on the phone were also in floods of tears. As I watched the conference on television, I saw that some Iraqi journalists were crying while others were screaming hysterically. The Americans on the platform were cock-a-hoop – but, standing in the background, the senior British diplomat, David Richmond, was a model of sensitive self-control.

The news broke early on a Sunday morning. A day before we had been praying in an all-night meeting that Saddam would soon be caught. We also prayed by name for some of the key people in the CPA and the military – every one of whom was standing on the platform at that triumphant press conference. Later that morning I was to preach at ANC, as both the pastors were away. I knew there would be great exultation and I knew I would be expected to comment on the events of the previous night. When the service began, the atmosphere was indeed charged. The worship was electric, people were dancing with joy – and I still felt awful. I didn't want to dampen the enthusiasm of the moment, but I felt that of all people I needed to be honest with this congregation.

I had already chosen as my text the first two verses of Hosea 6:

> Come, let us return to the LORD.
> He has torn us to pieces
>   but he will heal us;
> he has injured us
>   but he will bind up our wounds.
> After two days he will revive us;
>   on the third day he will restore us,
>   that we may live in his presence.

This certainly seemed appropriate for the occasion. In my sermon I talked frankly about the enormous pain of the day. I spoke of the hope of resurrection in this text and of its implications for the restoration of Iraq.

I spent the following day in Washington in a series of meetings in the State Department, before returning to Baghdad via Coventry – principally to pick up a crate of mince pies that the ladies of the cathedral had made for our diplomats in Iraq. (I also took them a Christmas card from the children of Bablake School, to stand alongside the one solitary 'Season's Greetings' the Bob

House had received from Jack Straw.) Even in Britain, where everything was much more muted, there was a sense of excitement in the air that maybe the capture of Saddam would be the turning-point for the new Iraq.

The following Sunday, I found myself preaching again at the Palace. The text for the day was the Magnificat, the song of Mary in the first chapter of Luke. Standing in front of Saddam's throne, I could not help but draw attention to this verse:

> He has brought down rulers from their thrones
> but has lifted up the humble.

Sitting on the throne that morning was one of the American military chaplains. I doubt that there could have been a better setting in the world in which to preach on that text that Sunday. Later that day, in St George's, I told the mainly Iraqi congregation of the setting of that morning's sermon, and for them too it was a cause of great rejoicing. On the altar in the chapel that morning we had placed the *chanukiah*, the eight-branched candelabrum used in the Jewish community to celebrate the miracle of Chanukah and commemorate Yehudah HaMacabee's victory over the Hellenistic forces that had desecrated the Temple in Jerusalem in 167 BC. There, the worship of the God of Israel had been replaced with the worship of idols. Here in Baghdad, the Chanukah of 2003 spoke of the triumph of good over evil. Here, in this place that had been at the heart of Saddam's monstrous rule, the worship of God was now taking place.

The capture of Saddam had certainly put one fear to rest, that the tyrant was coming back. Bizarre rumours had been circulating that on such-and-such a date he would be back in power. There were people I met who were afraid to give their full support to the Coalition because they feared that one day he might return. The news that Saddam had been recognized as a prisoner of war was not received so well. Thousands took to the streets shouting 'Death to Saddam!' They wanted to see him classed as a war criminal and executed as soon as possible. It was also clear that most Iraqis wanted him to be tried by Iraqis in Iraq.

My colleague Dr Mowaffak had been one of the four members of the Governing Council who had been taken to see Saddam on the morning of his capture, and just a few days later I met up with him. He had spent an hour with the prisoner and I was eager to discover how the conversation had gone. The four Iraqis had gone to see Saddam with Paul Bremer and General Ricardo Sanchez, the head of the Coalition forces in Iraq. The meeting was evidently very emotional. The Iraqis challenged Saddam with a list of the crimes he had committed. They asked him about the thousands who were buried in mass graves. He replied that they were all criminals and traitors. When they asked him about the use of chemical weapons in Halabja, he blamed it on the Iranians. Regarding the invasion of Kuwait, he continued to insist that it really belonged to Iraq. He was totally unrepentant. Dr Mowaffak described the experience as 'being in the presence of pure evil'. He stayed behind for a few minutes after the others had left, to tell Saddam that he was 'a wicked bastard' who would not be forgiven in this world or the next. Saddam is indeed illegitimate, and in Arabic society this is a source of the deepest shame. His response was a stream of anatomical abuse as Mr Bremer came back to fetch Dr Mowaffak away.

By now, there was a real sense that the country was in crisis – the original jubilation of a swift and effective war had waned and the Iraqis were very frightened that their country was descending into anarchy. And yet there was a sense too that a new shape was beginning to emerge out of the chaos. The work of rebuilding a nation is never easy, especially when it has suffered so severely for so long. The difficulty of doing it when under continual attack is phenomenal – and yet the commitment of the staff at the CPA was extraordinary. While most of the world was highly critical, I was full of admiration. Yes, they had made mistakes, but everyone had had a lot to master very quickly. In those first months after the war, things had been happening by the hour.

I had become familiar with much of the workings of the CPA and the Iraqi Governing Council. Both were made up of very impressive people working in extremely difficult conditions. The CPA had come a long way since the days when we found the Ministry of Justice under the stairs. Its role was to establish the new system for governing this large and widely dispersed nation. For each ministry there was a senior adviser and a team of people involved in recruiting and training the staff. A lot of energy was also being invested in involving the different communities, which included establishing local councils that would be a channel of communication between the people and the CPA and the Governing Council.

Even once the air-conditioning was working, the Palace was not the ideal building in which to house such a huge operation. To start with, Saddam didn't put in enough toilets, and the supplies of water and electricity were totally inadequate. Many of the fittings didn't work. Gold-plated taps may look very nice but if they don't work they are useless. Within a few months, the CPA had divided up all the ballrooms and the huge reception rooms with plywood into scores of offices. Some of the most crucial equipment was brought in from America, but most of the furniture was purchased locally. It was made in China and didn't last long.

Among the rickety Chinese furniture were the remnants of Saddam's soft furnishings, including some huge, ornate, deep-cushioned sofas. In the chaplain's office there was a collection of military helmets that belonged to Uday, the dictator's terrible son, and a couple of Saddam's swords. Frank Wismer also discovered two splendid inlaid lecterns, for which he found a new home in St George's. Over the four main entrances of the Palace towered the four enormous heads of Saddam, which seemed to be watching you wherever you went. They must have each been 20 ft high. Eventually they were taken down and chopped into little pieces, which were given to the CPA staff as souvenirs when they eventually left.

The meals are another thing I will never forget. To my mind Iraq has probably the best food in the world, but none of it came into the Palace. The kitchens were feeding nearly 4,000 people three times a day, and the fare was basic American, served on plastic plates with plastic knives and forks. It was awful – it made school dinners look like gourmet cuisine. At times we felt very nostalgic for the days immediately after the war, when we lived on the prepacked meals the soldiers ate.

We tried to ensure that our meetings with members of the Governing Council took place at lunchtime, as they would always take a lunch break and be served with wonderful Iraqi food. We would often sit down to eat with Iyad Allawi, Mowaffak al-Rubaie, Yonadam Kana, Ahmed Chalabi and other prominent figures, and at times it seemed a little strange to think that these were people making history and yet they were friends who we met almost daily. Their headquarters were less crowded than the Palace and far more Iraqi, and it was a relief to leave the Palace to visit them.

I was often called out late at night to try to resolve disagreement among the 25 members of the council. A curious feature of the politics of the new Iraq is the existence of two factions which had developed in exile in the London suburbs of Ealing and Wimbledon, and there were often tensions between them. There are political differences between these sets, and I have noticed that the Ealing Iraqis (who were led by Dr Mowaffak) tend to be much more religious than the other group; but as much as anything, the cause of the division between them was that, though in London they had lived only a few miles apart, they hadn't socialized with each other. Dr Allawi and his fellow doctor Ibrahim Ja'fari (who *is* a devout Muslim) both lived in Wimbledon.

I was also at the time working in Israel/Palestine, and this caused some disquiet. On one occasion, some members of the council told me I should be concentrating exclusively on their country. Somehow Yasser Arafat got to hear about this and when I was next in Ramalla he summoned both me and the Palestinian ambassador to Iraq. He got into one of his excitable moods. 'Father Andrew belongs here too', he told his ambassador, banging his fist on the table. 'He must not stop his work here. We need him just as much as Iraq.' The message got back to Baghdad. As one of the great champions of the Arab world, Mr Arafat was still revered in Iraq and his word was not questioned.

The Governing Council had been given the task of creating the body of basic law that would govern Iraq until the election. It was supposed to be ready by mid-December 2003, but it wasn't completed until the following March. It was published on International Women's Day – a day that was given huge significance in the new Iraq – and on the streets of Baghdad women danced in celebration of its signing. The temporary constitution gave women rights and freedoms that would have been applauded in any Western country but were as yet unique in the heart of the Islamic Middle East. It stipulated that women must hold at least a quarter of the seats in the new interim government, and at least a quarter of the seats in the elected national assembly.

Only two days later that joy was turned to terror in Baghdad as rockets pounded into the Green Zone. On one occasion I was thrown completely off my feet. But this was nothing compared to the agony and utter despair that followed the massacre of over 200 people on the Shia holy day of Ashura, at the holy shrine in Karbala and in the Baghdad neighbourhood of al-Kadamir. Bits of bodies were thrown into the air and people covered in blood wept uncontrollably beside the remains of their loved ones. Life in the new Iraq swung between elation and despair, and we were getting used to it. Whichever state you were in at the moment, you knew that the other was not far away.

Behind the scenes, people were working round the clock to try to ensure that this experiment of rebuilding a rogue state succeeded. Over a cup of tea in the IGC offices, Dr Mowaffak confessed to me that he hadn't seen a bed for three nights. He had been down in Najaf trying to persuade the Grand Ayatollah Ali Sistani to accept the draft constitution. Eventually he did so, albeit with great reluctance. Meanwhile, in Saddam's former presidential Palace the 3,850 staff of the CPA were at their desks from early morning until late at night. The more fortunate of them then went back to their shared trailers, while the less lucky slept in bunks in the Palace's makeshift dormitories.

Eventually the day arrived for the handover of sovereignty. I learned that I was to be one of the few Westerners to attend the ceremony at which the new Iraqi government would be presented. The venue for this was secret – we were to meet at 2 p.m. at al-Rashid within the Green Zone. I dutifully turned up on time, only to find that someone had just been firing mortars at the hotel and it was being evacuated. A group of Westerners, mainly diplomats, waited in the searing heat of the afternoon sun until we were put on a coach with curtains. I asked the driver if he knew where we were going and he said no, his instructions were simply to follow the military escort. After a short while, we ended up at the new supreme court, the place where it is believed Saddam will eventually be tried.

We waited in the corridors for another hour until the media arrived, herded in like a group of schoolchildren. They stood in line while their permits were checked and checked again and then they were led into the auditorium to the shouted instructions of the soldiers and the Coalition press team. Only when they were all safely in place behind their barrier were we allowed to take our assigned seats. Paul Bremer, General Sanchez and David Richmond were also present, but merely as guests.

Lakhdar Brahimi, the UN special envoy who had been charged with selecting the new government, entered the hall, followed by the 30 members of the new cabinet and the new President, Prime Minister and two Deputy Prime Ministers. It all looked so well planned and organized, but in reality it was not such a tidy event. It had been delayed a day because there had been a big disagreement over who should be the president. It was known that the CPA and the UN had wanted Adnan Pachachi, who had been Iraq's Foreign Minister before the Ba'thists seized power in 1968, but the Governing Council had insisted on Sheikh Ghazi al-Yawer. They had already announced, three days earlier, that they had chosen Iyad Allawi as the new Prime Minister.

And then the whole of the council resigned *en bloc* and handed power over to the new government. This was not how the transition was supposed to happen. In effect, the new government took power a month early. Dr Allawi was not Prime Minister elect or Prime Minister designate, he was Prime Minister for real. The CPA had been wrong-footed and it was a sign of its genuine loss of control.

After a series of eloquent speeches from Mr Brahimi, Sheikh al-Yawer and Dr Allawi, we chosen few withdrew to a reception.

It reminded me strangely of a bun fight in the church hall after the bishop has visited. Talking to the Prime Minister, I assured him that I had forgiven him for stealing the most trusted member of my team to be his chief spokesman. Meanwhile, Paul Bremer was standing in the corner with a cup of tea, looking a little forlorn. Only the day before, it had been him that everyone wanted to be photographed with. Now, it was the new President and Prime Minister.

The days that followed were days of great change. Mr Bremer was not irrelevant, but you could almost see the power slipping from his fingers, back to the Iraqi people. The mood on the street was optimistic as people were prepared to give the new government the benefit of the doubt. Even the fiery young radical Muqtada al-Sadr said that his followers should give it the chance to prove itself. Even so, it was clear that the transition to democracy was not going to be easy. Already there was a very marked increase in violence as those opposed to change made a last-ditch attempt to prevent it. The new leadership was desperate to convince the world that after 30 June Iraq would begin to control the growing anarchy on the streets. I'm not sure they really believed it themselves, but they knew they had to make a good show. The test will be whether the new Iraqi security services are able to get a grip.

Then came the week of the actual handover of sovereignty. It was my 40th birthday that week and we had arranged for a bit of a feast on 29 June, in a tented restaurant opposite the Palace. I had invited several diplomats to come and eat a sheep with us, including Mr Bremer and his team, and many of them had said they were coming. Then, the day before, we were told that the handover would take place in just one hour. Most people knew nothing about it when at 10.28 a.m. on 28 June Paul Bremer went with David Richmond to meet the new President and Prime

Minister, said the words, shook hands – and flew out of Iraq. I was in the Palace at the time and already people were moving the furniture out of the 'front office'. The Palace would henceforth be the American embassy, and the three rooms from which Iraq had been controlled for the past 15 months would now be the domain of the new ambassador.

Despite all the promise of the handover, there was a real sense of sadness. So many friends left immediately. So much of the expertise that had been assembled or accumulated by the Americans and the British was suddenly dispersed. Now we had to form new relationships and learn a new way of working. The change did not feel good.

Since that day, we have worked with Edward Chaplin, Britain's first formal ambassador to the new Iraq, and his American opposite number, John Negroponte, and have found them as able as anyone their countries have sent before. Meanwhile, the task that we face grows only more daunting. Iraq has become more dangerous than anyone who is not there can imagine. Life for the ordinary people has become intolerable. For most, the suffering is now far worse even than it was under Saddam. Many are beginning to feel hopeless. But we do not. We know that it is going to be a very long and very difficult business to restore peace to this nation, but we will not lose hope.

What is so special about Iraq?

As Iraq slips further towards possible civil war, and the world grows tired of stories of suicide bombs and beheadings, more and more people will be tempted to write off this land and condemn its people as barbarians, who failed to show any gratitude when they were liberated by a coalition of 28 other nations and have since repaid all the sacrifices made on their behalf with violence and incitement. Already the *Sun* newspaper has called them 'savages' who lack 'civilized standards'.

Yet this is anything but a barbarous country – or even a 'developing' one. Its people were sophisticated not just centuries but millennia before the tribes of Europe. However we interpret the biblical account which sets the Garden of Eden between the Tigris and the Euphrates, there is no disputing that this land has been a cradle of civilization. The water of those two great rivers, which turn the desert into a fertile valley, was once as rich a resource as the oil is today. 'Iraq' means 'deep roots', and Iraq is indeed the home of a nation with very deep roots. Its territory is not huge compared with its neighbours Iran, Saudi Arabia and Turkey, but it has seen a succession of dazzling cultures and today boasts more than 10,000 archaeological sites.

This country has played an important role in the history of all three of the great monotheistic religions. They all venerate the patriarch Abraham, who was born in the ancient capital of Sumeria, the city of Ur, near to present-day Nasiriya. This land is where the Jewish people were sent into exile, a shocking experience that inspired a new theology of salvation. The Torah probably took final shape in Babylon, and part of the Talmud was written there.

This land was also one of the places where Christianity first took root, when the Assyrians embraced the faith in the first century. The Chaldean Church still worships in a version of Aramaic, the language that Jesus spoke. And Iraq has also played a vital role in the development of Islam, and especially Shia Islam. It has the most sacred Shia shrines in the holy cities of Najaf and Karbala.

But its history stretches back much further than that. Almost 8,000 years ago, the people of Mesopotamia (literally 'Between Rivers') were growing crops, domesticating and keeping animals, and even painting. By 3000 BC, they had invented the wheel, developed a form of writing and built the world's first cities (giving rise to the biblical legend of the Tower of Babel). The *Epic of Gilgamesh* was composed a little later – one of the world's first great works of literature, which agonizes about what it means to be human.

Between 2371 and 2143 BC, the Akkadians created the first state that could be described as an 'empire'. They also invented the abacus. The Ur dynasty that followed was famous for its literature and its art. Hammurabi reigned from 1792 to 1750 BC and established one of the first known codes of secular law – a remarkably humane code which seeks to protect the weak and the poor, including women, children and slaves. It is regarded today as part of the foundations of modern law. After this, the Assyrians flourished in the north and built the great cities of Assure, Nineveh and Nimrud, whose remains are still visible today.

They were followed by the 'new' Babylonian period, from 612 to 538 BC, which gave Iraq the most significant name in its history: Nebuchadnezzar. It was he who constructed one of the seven wonders of the ancient world, the 'hanging' gardens. Just over a hundred years later, the Greek historian Herodotus recorded that Babylon surpassed in size and splendour any city in the known world. He said that most of its houses were three or four storeys high, and claimed that the outer walls were thick enough to allow a four-horse chariot to turn on their battlements.

We have the mathematicians of Babylon to thank for our calendar and the way we measure our days in 24 hours of 60 minutes and our circles in 360 degrees.

More than 1,000 years later, Iraq was once again the centre of the world's greatest civilization, as the Islamic empire spread from Spain and Morocco across north Africa to Arabia and beyond. In AD 762, the Abbasid caliph Abu Ja'far al-Mansur founded a new capital on the banks of the Tigris. It was originally called Madinat al-Salam, the City of Peace, but then became known as Baghdad. Four-and-a-half centuries later, the geographer Yakut al-Rumi described it thus:

Suburbs, covered with parks, gardens, villas and beautiful promenades, plentifully supplied with rich bazaars, mosques and baths, stretched for a considerable distance on both sides of the river. The population amounted to over two millions! Immense streets traversed the city. Every household was plentifully supplied with water at all seasons by the numerous aqueducts which intersected it; and the streets, gardens and parks were regularly swept and watered, and no refuse was allowed to remain within the walls. At night the streets were lighted by lamps. Along the wide-stretching quays lay whole fleets at anchor, sea and river craft of all kinds, from the Chinese junk to the old Assyrian raft resting on inflated skins. The mosques of the city were at once vast in size and remarkably beautiful. There were also numerous colleges of learning, hospitals, infirmaries for both sexes and lunatic asylums.

Throughout its heyday Baghdad was the intellectual centre of the world. Scholars of all races and religions were invited to work there. Great advances were made in astronomy, mathematics and medicine. The translation of ancient Greek writers such as Euclid and Aristotle into Arabic laid the foundations for the Renaissance in Western Europe. This was a refined culture that welcomed and preserved the best that the human mind had to offer. Baghdad was celebrated for its music and poetry. People played chess and backgammon.

Thereafter, this bright culture went into decline. In 1258, Baghdad was destroyed by the Mongols, led by the grandson of Genghis Khan. In 1534, Mesopotamia became part of the Turkish Ottoman Empire and at the end of the First World War it passed into British hands. Iraq achieved complete independence only in 1958, with the overthrow of the monarchy – and then ten years later the Ba'thists seized power.

The Iraqis are people of exceptional intelligence. Today, they have the opportunity once again to dazzle the world, if they can recover the secret of their past greatness: the extraordinary continuity of their civilization, which stretches back unbroken nearly 8,000 years, infused with the spirit of a generous, refined and tolerant Islam.

Chapter 11

Signs of new growth

In September 2004, when things were beginning to be really grim, I decided to ask every Iraqi I met in Baghdad a question: 'Given how dangerous and anarchic Iraq is now, don't you wish the war had never happened?' I phrased it in such a way that it would prompt them to say 'Yes'. But not one person agreed. The universal response was that they had to be liberated. It cannot be denied that it has been hard to keep hoping amidst the rising tide of violence and chaos – and yet it would be wrong to focus exclusively on all that is going wrong. The truth is that the situation today inspires both despair and hope. I have been honest about the agony of Iraq, but I trust I have also conveyed something of the sense of a nation being reborn. This is a country poised between fear and expectation.

The election on 30 January 2005 gave incredible hope to this beleaguered nation. Much of the world said that a fair vote was impossible and insurgents threatened to kill those who participated. Yet on that historic day people turned out in their millions – the young, the old, even the infirm. Real democracy was new to them. Before, there had always been only one name on the ballot paper: Saddam Hussein. Now, there were over 7,000 candidates and 120 political parties to choose from. Before, voting had been compulsory. Now, it was optional and yet, in spite of the danger, people queued at the polling stations for hours – and afterwards walked around, proudly holding up their index fingers, dyed purple to prevent fraud. More than 30 people were killed, and many thousands had their finger cruelly cut off, and yet the country was full of joy and full of pride. It was one sign of hope amidst the chaos.

The international media must take some blame for not showing how this country has been transformed. Despite the bloody resistance, there have been so many changes that have laid the foundation for the new Iraq. It can be immensely frustrating when the world is deaf to the stories of hospitals, schools and community facilities being rebuilt, or of the courageous Iraqi police who continue to turn up for work though their friends and colleagues are being targeted and killed. Despite the hardships of life in Iraq, it is still easier to feel hope there than it is in the comfort and safety of the West.

Ironically, some of the earliest improvements were in the media. In the old Iraq, there was no freedom of the press. The public had no access to satellite communications. Even the Internet was banned until just before the war. Now almost every main street has an Internet café and every home has a satellite dish. There are many new television channels and radio stations, and most of them do not put out the kind of propaganda that is the norm in so much of the Arab world. Meanwhile, the press has been liberated, with scores of new newspapers and magazines available.

You need to have been in Iraq in the old days to appreciate the transformation in its communications. Once, the only way to make an international phone call from Baghdad was to go to the Iraqi Airways office – and even there you would have to try many times before you could get a connection. Telecommunication with Iraq is still really bad, but it is getting better. There are now competing mobile-phone networks. One, on the American MCI system, was intended only for the Coalition and Iraqi officials but somehow the phones seemed to get into the hands of all sorts of people. There was considerable amusement in the Green Zone when it was discovered that even the pizza man had one. In Baghdad, there is another network called Iraqna. Admittedly it is a very poor service, but at least it exists. Now, we no longer have to rely on the expensive satellite service, we just struggle with the local mobile-phone network.

The renaissance of the Iraqi economy is something else that has received very little coverage. Before the war, Iraq was a very sorry place. Most of the shops were all but empty and only the privileged few could afford those commodities they did stock. Today, the shops in the major cities are filled with every product imaginable. What is more, people actually have the money to buy things. Before the war, people would earn between 3,000 and 9,000 dinars (that is, $2–$6) a month. Today, the incomes of those in work have risen to 300–600,000 dinars. Admittedly there has been considerable inflation and in many cities unemployment is very high, but the standard of living has improved greatly. As a result, people are spending money on restoring their damaged properties and vehicles and improving their workplaces – and this in turn has added to the wealth of their communities. Most people are eating much better. One obvious change in the markets has been the return of bananas. Saddam disliked this fruit and they were forbidden.

The oil industry is slowly being restored, despite the attempts by insurgents to destroy it, which have caused the country's first shortage. Petrol is now being sold at a more realistic price and as a result local enterprises are for the first time showing an interest in getting involved with an industry that is still the life-force of Iraq. Already, the multinationals are being consulted about the reconstruction of its infrastructure. Also, Iraq has the biggest untapped resources of natural gas in the world, and there are plans to exploit this and integrate this new industry with that of the neighbouring states. The old regime controlled the country's trade and stifled any real growth, but the new Ministry of Trade is working towards a free-market economy, liberating Iraq's private sector, which has been living without hope for the last 40 years. The Iraqi stock exchange has been revitalized and there is now active trade with many of the country's neighbours. Iraq was for a long time totally dependent on oil, but today its economy is increasingly mixed.

Just as Iraq's economy is being reconstructed, so too is its infrastructure. When I first visited Baghdad, the tap water burned my skin. Not so today. More than $1.6 billion has been allocated to the repair of 16 major water plants around the country – and not by NGOs such as Care International but by the new Ministry of Labour. The sewage system too is being restored. In days past, I used to watch children swimming amidst raw sewage in the Tigris. Now Baghdad is having its sanitation seen to for the first time in years, with the reopening of the city's main sewage works. Already, according to the World Health Organization, the incidence of diseases such as hepatitis B and C has decreased dramatically. It is hoped that very soon over 80 per cent of the city's drinking water will be treated and free from pathogens. Much of this work has been co-ordinated by the Coalition's military engineers.

The electricity supply was a major problem before the war and remains so, in part as a result of the damage insurgents have done to the oil industry. Efforts to repair it have been severely hampered since the very real threat of kidnap drove many foreign engineers out of the country. Yet even here there is hope. In areas of comparative calm, such as the northern, Kurdish governorates, the electricity supply has not only been restored, it has been privatized.

There have been considerable improvements in the transport infrastructure too. One of the last things Paul Bremer did before he left Iraq was to order a huge renovation of the streets of Baghdad. Almost overnight they were cleaned, their surfaces repaired, and the many traffic islands and roundabouts were painted and planted with flowers. Public transport is getting better, and Iraqi Airways is flying again for the first time in 13 years, with the prospect too of private investment.

The health of a nation is always a good measure of its welfare. The UN sanctions had had a devastating effect on the health of the Iraqis, even though Saddam's Minister of Health, Dr Umid Mubarak, was not only a physician but also a good man who really did care for the people. He did his best to maintain the health system and indeed had some real successes. In contrast, some of the CPA's medical policies were outrageous – not least its decision to scrap the bone marrow transplant centre on the grounds that it was a propaganda exercise by the old regime. After the handover of sovereignty to the Iraqis, the new Minister of Health put resources into the centre and allowed Dr Majid to resume his vital work as its director. Already nearly $1 billion has been allocated to the reconstruction of the country's health system. Existing hospitals are being repaired and new ones built. Within a few years Iraq could again have one of the best health-care systems in the Arab world.

Even in agriculture there is hope, though this is not without controversy. For years, under pressure from the sanctions, Iraqi farmers had been overcultivating their land and degrading their soil, resulting in poorer and poorer harvests. This is particularly true in the Mosul region, which historically has produced most of the country's wheat. The World Wide Wheat Company of Arizona has been helping farmers in the north to determine which seed will produce the best crops in that arid landscape, and it is possible that in the coming year Iraq may once more be self-sufficient in the principal cereals. At the same time, the American military has gone to great lengths to vaccinate many thousands of livestock.

Saddam oversaw a number of major ecological disasters. One of the worst of these was the destruction of the wetlands of southern Iraq. For over 5,000 years, a large community of Marsh Arabs had followed a unique way of life in that part of the country, living in houses built of reeds, on floating islands made of reeds, surrounded by an abundance of fish, birds and plants. Then, in 1991, in an exceptional show of courage, these people rose up against Saddam. His response was not only to slaughter them but to drain their marshes. The loss of this habitat was catastrophic. Now the dams and canals the Ba'thists built have been destroyed and already a fifth of the old marshland has re-appeared, along with its vegetation and wildlife. For the Marsh Arabs, this is a kind of resurrection.

But however important is the transformation of the economy, or of trade or infrastructure or health care, it is the educational system that assures the future of a nation. Under the old regime, children were abused by the system not only psychologically but also physically. Young David has countless scars, and when I asked him how he came by them he told me it was in the Saddam Fedayin, the Ba'thist equivalent of the Hitler Youth. Schoolboys would be made to take part in gruelling military exercises to prepare them to fight for their president and country. Those awful days are gone.

Millions of dollars are now being spent on restoring schools, colleges and universities. The school curriculum has been radically changed and most of the textbooks replaced. Even the university curricula are being revised. New alliances are being forged with universities overseas and it is hoped that one day Iraq will be secure enough for exchange schemes to operate. But still it has to be said that the present chaos in the country is preventing its education system from realizing its full potential. This is a nation that boasts many brilliant minds, yet it has never been able to fulfil its promise. My hope is that within a very few years it will.

Much more could be said about the signs of new growth in Iraq today, from the formation of an independent judiciary to the training of the fire brigade, but it is the new sense of freedom that gives real hope. Despite the chaos and the carnage, people are once again free to speak. They can criticize the government and the Coalition without having to fear for their lives. They can demonstrate on the streets and protest in the media without fear of reprisal. This is the reason why most Iraqis still say that they needed liberating and this is the reason why this great people will not lose hope for the future.

Chapter 12

A land of hope

For me, it has always been essential to maintain a hope that is both political and spiritual. At times when things are bad, I may give up political hope but I cling all the more to the spiritual. I often had this experience in my work in Israel/Palestine, but there I would simply walk down to the Church of the Holy Sepulchre and look into the empty tomb. There the story of the Resurrection would hold out to me the promise of a situation transformed. After Good Friday comes Easter. This is the hope that often I would cling to in Iraq.

While I have been in Baghdad, I have been writing a regular report for the *Church of England Newspaper*. Here is something I wrote at the beginning of May 2004, which conveys something of that spiritual hope that kept me going when all else failed:

> Life here continues to be difficult, to put it mildly. Last Tuesday morning, we were awoken by another bomb, this time at the 14 July Bridge. Six people were killed – five Iraqis and one American soldier. Many more were injured. I know most of the soldiers on that bridge – we go through this checkpoint several times each day.
>
> It took far longer than usual to enter the Palace on Tuesday – about two hours instead of ten minutes. Inside, everything was as normal. The fact that several people had been killed on their way into work in reality had very limited impact. Everybody continued to work at a punishing pace. Sadly, death and destruction are so much part of daily life here that they almost seem normal.

Meanwhile, the world was in uproar about the terrible pictures revealing a horrific story of abuse of Iraqi prisoners in the Abu Ghraib jail at the hands of Coalition troops. This has had a huge impact on the rest of the world but has had little impact here in Baghdad, until last Friday. On Friday, it was a major point preached on in many mosques. Here was the reason why the Coalition had failed to win the support of so many Iraqis, portrayed in a handful of pictures. If people had doubts about the Coalition before, these had provided the fuel to feed the flames of opposition. Amongst the Coalition staff, the story produced real shock and disbelief.

This week, [however, Ayatollah al-Sadr] gave a party to celebrate [the return of Sheikh Abdel Latif to Iraq]. This in itself was a historic event – a leading Shia ayatollah entertaining a leading Sunni cleric who was part of the old regime. The dinner was a picture of the hope of the new Iraq – a hope based on forgiveness. As I often say, forgiveness is the only thing that will prevent the pain of the past from determining the future. The ayatollah has forgiven the sheikh and as they sat they discussed how together they might work to build the new Iraq.

Last week I took Sheikh Abdel Latif into the Palace. As he sat with other Sunni sheikhs and the leaders of the CPA, once again he spoke of his desire to help to bring peace to the new Iraq. At the same time he acknowledged that he was on trial. In his defence he stated that he had been misunderstood. Richard Jones, Mr Bremer's deputy, responded that we had all been misunderstood.

Without being here it is very difficult to assess what is really going on. There is so much pain that you have to put up a shield to protect yourself from it, and yet at the same time there are also many signs of hope. Forgiveness is being shown on all sides and the fragile plan for restoring order to Falluja is a sign of this. So, amidst the chaos, we must not lose hope.

This was written on a bad day, but it indicates where we looked for both political and spiritual hope. Yes, things have deteriorated in terms of law and order – certainly, what ensued in Falluja six months later was very grim – but the leaders of the new Iraq are full of hope. They are convinced that eventually they will restore their country to its former glory – not the glory of the days of Babylon's power that Saddam harked back to, but that of the days when Baghdad was the centre of the known world and a brilliant beacon of science and culture. In the election of 30 January 2005, the Iraqi people began at last to take control themselves of their country and its future. They are not prepared to allow the renegade Ba'thists or the religious militants to destroy it.

These things allow me still to be optimistic, but the most enduring hope for me lies in the character of the people and my conviction that God is still on their side. I have always considered the highlight of each week in Baghdad to be the worship at St George's on Sunday afternoon. When we held that first service of thanksgiving for the liberation of Iraq, the small congregation consisted largely of American and British diplomats and soldiers. Within a matter of weeks, the church was full of Iraqis. By Christmas, we regularly had more than 200 adults and 100 children. The building, which had just been a shell, had been cleaned outside and painted inside, its windows reglazed and its doors rehung. Today the church has chairs, a carpet and an electric piano, and the liturgy and the hymns are projected onto a screen at the front.

The congregation consists mainly of poor Christians – Chaldeans, Assyrians, Presbyterians – but there are also Muslims who attend, because they find there a sense of community and a reverence for God (and also, I suspect, because St George is venerated throughout the Arab world, and especially in Iraq). The needs of these people are immense and we try to help as many as we can. One Sunday, one couple came to me in tears. Two of their five children had been shot in the head, simply because their father made wine. He showed me photographs of these beautiful young children, gunned down in their own home. They were the most horrific pictures I had ever seen. There will be no inquiry and no justice for this family. Their only place of shelter, their only source of help and hope, is the church.

The missionaries who poured into the country as soon as the war was over have now all gone – Iraq is too dangerous for foreigners. St George's, however, grows from strength to strength – a caring community of people who are desperate to know more of God and his love. It is a very poor church, because we have little funding and no security, and yet it is one of the richest churches I have ever been part of. What we have is an assurance that somehow God will provide and a love that binds us together in adversity.

Every Sunday, after the service, we have cake and cold drinks on the church lawn, between two bombed-out government buildings, and talk about the week's events. People come asking for advice and help, we hug each other and at times shed tears together at the news of the death or injury of someone in the congregation in the latest violence. In some ways it is like any other Anglican church on a Sunday – except that none of these people are Anglicans and it is at least 50°C. Finally a bus arrives to take them all home, as it is too dangerous for people to travel alone, even though most of them live close by. When I ask them why they come to St George's, they tell me that it is because they find God there.

There have been many highlights in the life of the church, but nothing quite compares to both the joy and the seriousness of Palm Sunday 2004, when the cries of 'Hosanna!' rang through the streets of Baghdad and the prayers of the people for God to save them were expressed with real passion. Pentecost was another highlight, as we gave thanks to God for sending the Comforter, the Holy Spirit. We also celebrated the birthday of the church with a huge, seven-tiered cake. Every crumb was eaten. There are many challenges that lie ahead for St George's, but it has been a beacon of light and hope to a nation in despair.

Returning to Baghdad after the war, I had such a sense of the presence of God as I had experienced nowhere else. On one day I wrote in my diary:

> I have seen God's glory over Baghdad, like a cloud sur-
> rounding the city, and the last few days the glory has been
> increasing. At times it is as if we are walking in the taber-
> nacle of the Lord. His *Shechinah* glory is here. Hour after
> hour we are aware that there is a supernatural anointing
> over our work. God throws open all the doors that we need
> to go through. There is an ease in the presence of God, there
> is no struggle. We simply ask God to act and he does in
> ways beyond our comprehension.

I felt that God was still present and active in this land where he had once revealed his purposes through his prophets. I began thinking in particular about Ezekiel, for it was in Iraq that God spoke through him of the glory that filled the Temple in Jerusalem (Ezekiel 43.1–5). That glory came from the east – from Babylon – and the vision of it was like the one the prophet had seen by the river Kebar, by a town called Tel Abib where the Hebrew exiles were living in present-day Iraq. This spiritual hope spurred me to find out more about what became of Ezekiel. I knew he was buried in Iraq, but I didn't know where.

After some investigation, I discovered that his final resting place was in al-Kifl – which is Arabic for 'Ezekiel' – just north of Najaf. Early one Friday morning, we set off on the journey south. Georges was driving and Tom was with us. We travelled for three hours, through the ancient city of Babylon until we came to the old and derelict town of al-Kifl. We asked people along the road how to get to the tomb, and in return we received not just directions but panegyrics about how holy this place was. One man told us we must take our shoes off when we got there, because this is what God told Musa (Moses) to do when he was on holy ground.

As we arrived in the town we were caught in a terrible traffic jam, like I had never experienced before. Ours was the only car – all the other 'vehicles' were donkeys. Eventually we escaped their wrath and drove on, over open sewers, until we reached the holy place. The path to the tomb led through the courtyard of a 900-year-old mosque and into that of a classically beautiful Oriental synagogue, complete with palm trees and a well. There was a real sense of the presence of God here. This was one of the oldest synagogues in the world, built around AD 500 on a site where the tomb of Ezekiel had already been revered for 1,000 years.

Inside the synagogue we found Muslims praying, and there in the middle was the tomb. Around the top of the wall were written in Hebrew some verses from Ezekiel 43. It was a quite phenomenal experience. The glory of the Lord was there. I looked up at the ceiling, which was highly decorated with Jewish art which must have been several hundred years old, and there I saw in Hebrew the words 'Glory to the Lord'. I didn't want to leave this place when we had to go. On our way out, we were shown four other tombs, which the warden explained belonged to friends of Ezekiel, one of whom supposedly brought the Torah from Jerusalem to Babylon. As we stood in the courtyard in the glorious sunshine, the warden spoke of his joy at our visit. He was a Shia Muslim and yet he talked with great affection about both Jews and Christians. He asked me if I would return to take a Christian service by the tomb. I said that I would.

On the way back to Baghdad, we stopped off at Babylon. When I last visited three years before, I had been taken there by the Mukhabarat. It seemed to me an evil place and I had wanted to get away as soon as possible. Today, it is the base of the 1,700 Polish troops in Iraq. Our CPA passes got us in and it helped that Georges could communicate with the soldiers in Russian. We went into Saddam's palace – one of the most beautiful of the 68 he built for himself – and saw how he had had his initials inscribed on every brick, as Nebuchadnezzar had done in the city opposite over 2,500 years before. Walking around the empty, looted building, it seemed to us that there was something strangely biblical about the fall of this new Babylon.

A few hours later, as we approached the outskirts of Baghdad, the engine of our car suddenly started to splutter, as if we were running out of petrol. Behind us was a convoy of 20 petrol tankers from Kuwait, and we became concerned that we were holding them up. Seconds later, a bomb exploded in front of us. It was because our car had stuttered and slowed that neither we nor the tankers behind us (which must have been the target) were blown up. Our car then started working fine. It was as if angels had come with us to protect us on the journey – a journey of hope into the depths of the biblical history of Iraq.

The Bible is full of references to this land, from the creation story in Genesis 2 to the prophecies against Babylon in Revelation 17–18. In between, there is the story of the Tower of Babel in Genesis 11. Genesis also tells us that the patriarch Abraham came from Ur (chapter 11) and his daughter-in-law from Nahor (chapter 24), and his grandson Jacob spent 20 years in what is now Iraq. This was where the Hebrews were sent into exile and was thus the home of Daniel and many of their other great men. It was to the city of Nineveh (on the edge of modern-day Mosul) that Jonah was sent by God as a reluctant evangelist to warn the Assyrians of coming judgement. It was in this land that the events of the Book of Esther took place. It was this land that was the target of Nahum's damning prophecy. The only land mentioned more frequently in the Bible is Israel/Palestine.

Much in this history is negative – but the positive thing is that God never deserts his faithful people in this land. So, however bad the present situation may seem, there is hope in Iraq: political, economic, social and spiritual. The restoration of this great nation will take time. There are those who will try to frustrate it, but they will not succeed. The people of Iraq will not allow them to do so. Both their political and their spiritual leaders are committed to building a generous, just and democratic society. They are committed to transforming the land of the Tigris and the Euphrates. And, with the help of the international community, they will do so. In the words of Ayatollah al-Sadr, the sun has risen again over Iraq. Even though at times it may seem hidden, we know that its full radiance will shine on this land again.

Chapter 13

The darkness and the glory

Eighteen months have passed since I wrote the previous chapter. In those days I could still speak about specific acts of violence and individual tragedies, but now the slaughter is so unremitting it is almost impossible to write about anything particular. I have spent much of my life in war zones and my observation has generally been that what is shown on television looks far worse than the reality. The opposite is true of Iraq. What we see on our TV screens is a tiny fraction of the present carnage. I used to be quite critical of the media, but I acknowledge that their task now in Iraq is almost impossible. Over a hundred Western journalists have been killed already, and several thousand Iraqis.

Peter Maki now travels with me as my special assistant from HQ. I told him on his first visit to Baghdad not to worry about an alarm clock, as we are awoken almost every morning by the huge shudder of a bomb going off or a rocket landing. Electricity is far scarcer than it was in the early days after the war – indeed, all basic services are worse, not better. The other day, Mrs Samia, now a member of the Iraqi parliament, told me she finds it hard even to take a bath, because she knows the water comes from the Tigris and every day so many bodies are thrown into it. I confess I hadn't thought of that when I took a shower each day. The river that was once the life force of this country is now polluted by death and destruction. Daily I hear of scores of fresh human corpses discovered in this city, and when a dozen heads are found I know the bodies are probably floating in the Tigris. Huge numbers have been killed – many, many more than the media report. We are told about so many dead in a suicide car bombing, but there is no mention of the doctors who were shot dead on the way home from the hospital. I would guess that at least half a million have died as a result of violence since the war, though there is no way of knowing.

In Chapter 11, I mentioned that on every visit I used to ask every Iraqi I met: 'Don't you wish the war had never happened?' The answer was always 'no' – until January 2006. Then, everything began to change. At first people were uncertain, but then they began to acknowledge that things are now so bad that it was actually better under Saddam. Then they could at least send their children to school in safety. They could at least go to the market, even if there was often no food there. Now they don't know who is going to try to kill them or when they are going to strike. Every week, I ask my Iraqi congregation what they want to tell me and people say, 'I went to the market and the woman next to me was shot dead' or 'A car bomb went off and I just managed to escape the fire.' Something has gone very wrong. I have even asked myself whether I was right to support the invasion of Iraq so strongly in the first place. I will come back to this later.

Nor has my team been exempt from the violence. In the 12 months after September 2005, 11 of my colleagues were killed – every one of the leaders at St George's, as well as one of the church's guards, and several members of my hostage negotiation team. All of them were people I loved, people I shed tears for. Recently when I phoned Mrs Samia, she was weeping. Gunmen had burst into her house and killed three of her relatives. Her niece, who survived the attack, had been shot in the face, the arms and the legs, and her stomach had been cut open with a knife. At the US Army hospital where she was taken, the doctors had had to remove both her eyes. Nonetheless, this young Muslim woman wrote in a letter: 'God gave me sight for 30 years. I feel no anger that it has been taken away. It is God's will.' Today, the terrorists are living in Mrs Samia's house – yet even now she insists that she will not give up the struggle for peace.

The violence and chaos are being perpetrated by the same people I listed earlier, but the number of groups involved has increased. As I expected, the death of Abu Musab al-Zarqawi in an American air strike in June 2006 did not make any difference, though it was greeted with jubilation. There were so many people ready to take over from him, and in fact al-Qa'ida's part in the bloodshed, which at first was quite small, has grown bigger since his removal. Meanwhile, both Muqtada al-Sadr's Mehdi Army and the rival Shia militia of Sciri have grown in strength, and there is increasing tension between them as a turf war develops. There is also more and more interference from outside Iraq – not least from its neighbours Syria and Iran.

A new concern has been the emergence of death squads within the police and the Ministry of Interior. The new Prime Minister, Nouri al-Maliki, is totally opposed to this, but the Iraqi government is not a coherent body and each individual department does its own thing. To some extent the organs of the state have been infiltrated by insurgents, but it is also the case that senior members of the government are using their ministries to pursue sectarian aims.

The religious element in the terrorism has grown, not diminished, and yet there has still been no concerted effort from the Coalition to deal with this. Violence in God's name is something that most people have been afraid to acknowledge. In the immediate aftermath of the war, while the CPA was running the country, there was almost a feeling that if everyone ignored religion it wouldn't cause any trouble. I told anyone who would listen that we ignore religion at our peril, but though there were a few in the CPA who accepted this, most did not. Sadly, my worst fears have been realized.

It is very clear that people are trying to create more and more

mayhem in Iraq, though I don't believe that anyone wishes to pre-
cipitate all-out civil war. In the end, people resort to violence in
order to demonstrate that they have power. The Sunna have lost
the privileged position they enjoyed under Saddam, and killing
the Shia is the only way they feel they can reassert themselves. The
Shia retaliate, but also – like the former Ba'thists – they want to
drive the Coalition forces out of their country. Al-Qa'ida wants to
persuade the West that its whole approach to Islam is wrong.

There are also serious efforts at 'ethnic cleansing', as each community tries to turn its neighbourhood into a stronghold, free from
'the other'. Almost every day people who live in the 'wrong' area
tell me they have been ordered to leave. Often, a bullet is delivered
to their house as a warning. Although the fear and hatred between
Shia and Sunna have been exacerbated by the recent atrocities, I
believe they were always there, though suppressed under Saddam.
Before the invasion, people were forever assuring me, 'We are all
the same,' but I always felt they were 'protesting too much'.

Has Iraq already descended into civil war? The answer to that
depends on how you define civil war. When the major Shia shrine
in Samara is blown up and scores of people are killed, and then
dozens of Sunni mosques are attacked and scores more people
die, it certainly looks like civil war to me. But to admit this is also
a political statement, and it is amazing to see how many people
who are political allies have disagreed on this question. On all
sides there are calls for the Coalition to withdraw its forces and
leave the Iraqis to sort out their problems by themselves, but I
dread to think what would ensue if this happened.

Despite all this, however, I still love to be in Baghdad. I ask
myself: Why? Am I just some mad, maverick priest or is there
some deeper reason? I have to acknowledge that most people are
not like me. There is not one non-Iraqi I work with who has been
in the country as long as me. Very few foreigners even visited

Iraq before the war. I remember those days well: being watched continually, accompanied by spies all day and knowing there was a man outside the door of my hotel room all night. I remember well the intense fear I saw in every ordinary Iraqi I met – and, yes, even I was fearful then. Certainly, they were not the good old days for me. For me, those were the first few months after the liberation of Baghdad, when I could walk its streets, drink in its tea houses and eat good local food with the little children who became my friends. How I long for those days again!

When I was first asked if I would go to Saddam's trial – not the major trial now under way for the massacre of Kurds in 'Operation Anfal', but the earlier one for his reprisals against the Shia of Dujail – I wasn't sure what to say. My memory leapt back to the day he was found, to the jubilation of the Americans and the anguish of the Iraqis. I recalled my own tears as I realized how much pain this wicked man had caused. In the end, I decided to go. Early in the morning, we were taken to the court in one of the armoured buses known as 'rhinos'. The security was immense: five rounds of exhaustive screening and X-rays, and all our equipment taken away except for a pen and paper. After a very long time, we were taken into the little courtroom. And then he entered. The man the Iraqi people had feared for so long – whom I had feared for so long – was there, just a couple of yards away from me. I had always wondered how I would react if I ever saw him, and as I think about it now I realize that I was quite frightened.

At first I had no thoughts, I simply felt that I was in the presence of pure evil. He looked at me and I looked at him and we held each other's gaze for several minutes. After that, he kept turning round and staring at me. Did he recognize me from my countless appearances on Iraqi TV before the war? I couldn't tell, and couldn't ask him. My mind was numbed, and in fact I was several hours in the courtroom before I could think rationally. I remember wondering how come this old man had been allowed hair dye in prison. Apart from his beard, there wasn't a single grey hair on his head. There was always a copy of the Qur'an in his hand, though in all his years as ruler of Iraq he had never followed a single one of its precepts. On subsequent visits to the court, I listened to the stories of the suffering he was accused of inflicting. I knew it was just a very small part of what the people had endured. The more time I spent in that room, the more aware I was of the presence of evil.

Then, one day, who should appear as a witness for the defence but Tariq Aziz? For some reason – I never found out why – he turned up in his pyjamas. I didn't want him to see me, though I can't really work out why. I had spent so many hours with him before the war and he would certainly have recognized me; but why I felt it necessary to leave the room while he gave evidence I can't say. In Iraq, you don't always know why you react as you do.

It was the beginning of November 2006 when the verdict of this first trial was announced. Saddam was sentenced to death by hanging. It was a difficult day. The Shia celebrated and the Sunna marched in the streets, threatening more violence. Each community fired rockets at the other. For me, there was no rejoicing, as the pain of those years of oppression flooded back. The media pursued me for comments, and many of them told me what they wanted me to say: that the trial was flawed and that the sentence was wrong and was only going to provoke more chaos. I didn't agree with any of these claims, which made life rather difficult.

Many commentators saw the mid-term elections in America as a referendum on the ever-worsening situation in Iraq. The outcome was not what most of their military in Iraq wanted: the Democrats took control of both the House of Representatives and the Senate. The following day, Donald Rumsfeld resigned from his post as Secretary of Defense. I thought his departure would have a major impact on the ground in Baghdad and was surprised to find that in fact its effect was minimal. Some of the senior American officers even said they thought it was a good thing. One thing was undeniable: everything was going wrong. The carnage was increasing daily, the Iraqi government was not functioning well and in the countries in the Coalition – not least, America – the general public was seriously distressed by the character of the conflict.

Had the war really been necessary? I still say yes. I hadn't found it easy attending Saddam's trial, but just hearing how he and his regime had made people suffer had convinced me all over again that they had to be removed. Did we do everything right after the liberation of Iraq? I am afraid not. Many mistakes were made in those early days besides the failure to close the country's borders and the decision to dismiss all its security services. When the CPA was dissolved on 27 June 2004 and control was handed over to the Iraqis, they were not ready to take over – as many of them now admit. Running an opposition party in exile is not the same as governing one of the most complex societies in the world. One thing the British learned in their years of empire is that if you take over a country you should not leave too soon.

I think it was also a major mistake to try to impose Western-style democracy. It doesn't work in this part of the world. Think of the most stable countries in the region, such as Jordan and Morocco: essentially, they are benevolent dictatorships. Another error was not to involve Iraq's religious leaders sufficiently. Even before the invasion I was saying that unless they were properly engaged in the efforts to reconstruct their country, there would be a descent into violence and chaos. I cannot forget the letter I received from the British Foreign Office at the start of 2003 telling me that religious issues could not be attended to until the water and electricity supplies had been sorted out. Today, water and electricity are still scarce and it is widely recognized that religion is a large factor in most of the sectarian conflict.

On the other hand, although there has been some misconduct by Coalition soldiers, many of them have been outstanding. Recently I saw a graffito in the American embassy in Baghdad that said: 'If you don't want to stand behind your troops, stand in front of them.' How true! There are not many people who can keep going when they are under constant attack and regularly see their colleagues being killed. Despite all these difficulties, the military are still doing excellent reconstruction work when they can, building schools and hospitals, restoring power supplies and upgrading water systems. (All the civil construction companies, having been paid millions and millions of dollars, have now left the country.) Sadly, little of this is being done in Baghdad: it is far too dangerous.

The longer I have spent in Iraq, the more respect I have gained for the military. Their job is so critical, and yet they are so misunderstood. Much of the world sees them as the principal cause of Iraq's problems, a clumsy and dangerous instrument that is only exacerbating the violence. The people I see, however, are committed and highly professional – and ready to sacrifice their lives. Many are reservists who are willing to give up a year or more to fight for the freedom of a nation they knew very little about. I know many of them particularly well through chapel and church activities – men such as Colonel Tim Curran, who runs the Anglican service in my absence, and Commander Jeff Torrence of the US Navy, who leads worship in the evangelical service. The latter was once a member of St Andrew's, Chorleywood, the church that is probably my biggest supporter in Britain. Both of them are outstanding men, working far away from their families to help to rebuild Iraq.

I have also been struck by the way that in Britain we all but forget our soldiers. In America it is very different: most people respect their troops, and the churches pray for them and their safety. Sadly, the only time I have heard a prayer for our soldiers in a British church was on Remembrance Sunday. Just one day in November. There is a distinct lack of awareness that today the military are in the front line of peacemaking and peacekeeping. Despite all the negativity about the military, my faith in them has not diminished but actually increased. I am in a minority, but I do spend much of my time with them.

One of the areas we continue to work in is the field of hostage negotiations. Not so much has been heard about this lately, but that doesn't mean that the situation has improved. In fact, it has continued to get worse. Not so many Westerners are abducted now, but this is because there are now very few Westerners outside the Green Zone. Things have become so dangerous that people no longer go there – and, dare I say, should no longer go there. The vast majority of hostages taken now – and it is often scores of people each day – are Iraqi. Most of them are kidnapped for financial rather than political reasons. People can no longer send their children to school, because they may not return. The richer you are, the greater the risk. As a result, many professional people have fled the country. The hospitals are increasingly short of doctors, and the universities of lecturers. The situation is desperate.

Hostage work is always very fraught and it has often ended in tears, though sometimes in joy. Nonetheless, we have to do it. In recent months I have worked on the cases of all the Western hostages. As always, this has been difficult and dangerous, and some Iraqi members of my team have been killed in the process. Sadly, some of those who have been abducted have been people I urged to leave if they didn't want to be kidnapped and killed. They didn't leave, and they ended up dead.

Working on Iraqi cases is very different from Westerners – it more often involves money – but it is not always easier. On one occasion, however, the staff at St George's contacted me to say that one of our guards had been kidnapped. We immediately opened negotiations, only to be told that his abductors had wanted a Shia and, now they had looked at his ID and realized that he was a Christian, we could have him back. This must be one of the few cases in the Middle East when being a Christian was actually an advantage.

Many people have drawn attention to the particular suffering of Christians in Iraq. Priests have been attacked, and acid has been thrown in the faces of women not wearing veils. Christians make up only 5 per cent of the population, but account for 40 per cent of those who have fled the country since the end of the war. Many others have taken refuge in the north. Those who are attacking them seem not to realize that Christianity took root in the Middle East long before Islam – that indeed it originated there. Another problem is that Christians are regarded as being in league with the 'occupying' forces. In 2004 we had to take down the sign that identified St George's as Anglican in order to distance the church from the Coalition. The situation is indeed desperate.

Nonetheless, though the threats against Christians are real and great, we have to be careful not to exaggerate or exacerbate the situation. We need to remember that everyone in Iraq is suffering, whether they are Sunni, Shia, Turkman, Kurd or Christian. Most of the other communities are much larger, and so the number of attacks on them is much greater. In fact, far more mosques have been destroyed by bombs than churches.

I no longer work for the International Centre for Reconciliation or the Iraqi Institute of Peace, but am active in Iraq now as president of the Foundation for Relief and Reconciliation in the Middle East, which I launched in June 2005 with the former archbishop of Canterbury Lord Carey. I still spend much of my time in Baghdad, but the international zone now seems more like America than Iraq. Recently I was invited to act as chaplain to

Congress in Washington DC, an honour no Englishman had had since the Revolution of 1775. I said it must be because I work in the 51st state of America: the Green Zone in Baghdad.

I have met all of Iraq's prime ministers since the overthrow of Saddam and known them all, from the secular relativism of Iyad Allawi to the great historical knowledge of Ibrahim Ja'fari to the quiet and benign authority of the current Prime Minister, Mr al-Maliki. I have liked them all. They have been very different, but all three have respected what I and my colleagues are trying to achieve – and all have asked more of us. Recently when I discussed things with Mr al-Maliki, he agreed that religion was a major factor in the violence. The pressure on him now is enormous. He has one of the hardest jobs in the world, and his government does not have all the resources it needs, or the know-how. There are no simple solutions to anything. Everything will take time, and plenty of it.

The role of Dr Mowaffak has continued to expand and become more complex. He remains the National Security Adviser, and my closest colleague in the Iraqi government. I respect him and trust him completely. Whenever the premiership has become vacant, I confess, I have hoped the position would go to him. I still think it is a real possibility. He still runs the Iraqi Institute of Peace, but he also sits on the board of the FRRME and is chairing our new initiative to deal with religious sectarianism in Iraq.

The work of the IIP has continued, though it has not been easy. Its use of the Centre has been seriously restricted as the violence and chaos in Baghdad have grown, and it has also gone through some difficult changes of leadership. Fadel had to leave the country in 2005 because there was such a huge price on his head, and he now works for the FRRME in England and Jordan as my Iraq director. Nonetheless, the IIP has played an active role in the various elections and has co-operated closely with the UN; and its six working parties have persevered, though even their work has become more complex. The US Institute of Peace rapidly became its main source of both funds and training. What the long-term future of the IIP will be, I don't know; but certainly there is a desire to continue its work.

One major development has been that we now co-operate more closely with the American military. This is something else I would never have envisaged 20 years ago: that I would be sitting down with soldiers, working out strategies to reduce sectarian violence and increase engagement with religious leaders. At last this issue is being taken seriously, and one of our biggest supporters on this front is the Pentagon, which seems to have grasped the idea that if religious leaders lie behind much of the violence, it is essential to enlist their help in bringing it to an end. We have begun working especially closely with American military chaplains. This has been new for them, too – the team led by the most senior US Army chaplain in Iraq, Mike Hoyt, had never been involved in this kind of thing before. Colonel Hoyt proved to be an invaluable help, taking time to explain to us how the military thought and worked.

By November 2006, the Pentagon and the Iraqi government had together given us the contract to tackle the religious roots of the sectarian violence and had undertaken to finance this. This is the largest source of funding the FRRME has received, but it is also our biggest task: to work out how religious leaders can work with the military in a holistic approach to peacemaking. It is a mission made in hell, but I believe it is the only way to achieve peace and I am trying to address it with the same courage and determination that soldiers show in times of war.

In the midst of the continuing bloodshed in Iraq, it has often been my weekend work that has kept me going. At St George's we have also faced tragedy. On 12 September 2005, Maher and his

family and the other church leaders were due to return from a
conference in Amman. Over a year later, they have still not come
home. Other members of our staff and many of the congregation
have been killed, yet the church continues to grow and it is one of
the most dynamic congregations I have ever been part of. The
building itself is unscathed, though it is surrounded by concrete
barricades and razor wire. I haven't been able to visit it for two
years now, as it lies outside the protection of the international
zone, and when I am in the country we meet in the Prime
Minister's office. Most of the security guards there now are from
South America, and as good Catholics they love to join us for
Communion and we love them being there. I am sure we are the
only church in the world that meets in the office of a Shia Muslim,
and I often describe this as interfaith relations at the cutting edge;
and Mr al-Maliki agrees.

The following is one of the fortnightly 'spiritual updates' I send
my supporters, from August 2006. It gives a real insight into
my ministry in Baghdad and the life of worship that keeps me
going:

Yes, everything is awful in this part of the world and I have
been very nearly killed twice in the past week – but this is
not about the bad but the good. Because God is here in Iraq
and I love it.

I have written about how I have seen God's glory in Iraq.
It has increased, and is incredible. What we are seeing every
day is so amazing I am almost lost for words. I am going to
tell you mainly about one weekend. Saturday is mainly
devoted to my Iraqi congregation. We leave at 10am for the
Prime Minister's office. It is taking longer than ever to get
the people through security and yesterday it took about
three hours, so we spent the first couple of hours just

singing. Many children turned up, too, which was great. I
sent [my right-hand man] Samir off to the military shop to
buy them sweets and he returned with four carrier bags full.

I looked around the congregation. What wonderful
people they are! I love them so much. All of them have
suffered so terribly. Many have lost loved ones; all have lost
friends. The children are more than wonderful, and they
sang to us all so beautifully. I told them the story of Daniel
in the lions' den: they knew it very well – and knew it
happened just down the road. Amongst the children was
little Vivian, a girl of six who has terrible bladder cancer.
How I pray for this little girl! David tells me that whenever
she goes to the church she kneels in front of the altar and
prays and prays. She sits with the daughter of a member of
our staff who was recently killed, and in their young beauty
they look quite heavenly.

Also at the service was Phil, an Australian officer, and an
American contractor called Lane, who both spoke to the
congregation for a while. Then we sang some more, and I
preached about Daniel seeing the Son of Man over the
Tigris in Daniel 10. We sang some more, and then it was
time to commission our two new lay leaders, Majed and
Faiz, both wonderful men of God. All the children laid
hands on them as well as Phil and Lane and I, and we
anointed them. Then, after Eucharist, we baptized a new
baby, Rula, and that too was wonderful. Also in the congregation were four Iraqis from the same family, two men and
two women, who wanted to become Christians. In the
service it was as if something of heaven came down and
touched us. This may be a poor congregation in a highly
dangerous area, but these people just pour out the glory of
God with joy.

After the service, I sat in the corner and heard people's stories. Some hadn't eaten for several days, others had received death threats, others were ill – and then Vivian's father came. He showed me a letter from the hospital, which said that her cancer had progressed, there was nobody who could operate on her and the radiotherapy machine no longer worked, so she couldn't get any treatment.

We left the service nearly seven hours after we had arrived. It had been a deeply moving service, so powerful – but all through the night I was so distressed about Vivian. Even getting people to Britain now for treatment is near impossible. The cost would be enormous, too, even if we only took her to Jordan. I just needed a good urologist, with the right equipment.

Sunday began with the evangelical service in the Palace. One of our readings was Romans 8.35ff, that nothing, not even death, can separate us from the love of Christ. It was read by Captain French of the US Navy. His mother had died just a few hours before, but he still read his reading and also played the drums. I spoke on the subject of worship, and how in worship heaven comes to earth and we are taken up into heaven. The service was quite won-derful, but I was still thinking of little Vivian. After it ended, I stood at the door talking to people. An American officer came up to me and said he was born in England. I asked him where and it was only ten miles or so from where I now live in Hampshire. I asked him what he was doing in Baghdad and he replied, 'Oh, I'm just a urologist at the CSH' – the US Army combat support hospital. 'Just a urologist!' I said. 'You are the one man in the world I needed to meet right now.'

I told him about little Vivian, and without hesitation he

said he would treat her and I should take her to see him at the military hospital the next morning. I have spoken to him three times since then and have read him her notes, and he just so happens to specialize in the very type of cancer she is suffering from. This is a miracle, a miracle bigger than the 43 lorries full of meat: that in the chapel in the Palace in Baghdad an eminent urologist should come up to me who is in Iraq on reserve duty for several more months. Vivian will now be treated a mile from her home in a perfect American hospital.

When I took the Anglican service next, I was so excited I could hardly contain myself. The service was great. Afterwards, I met with the church council and then I prepared for the evening service. In the evening, we must have had over 200 people. The atmosphere was electric, the place was buzzing and the praise was the very best I have ever experienced. When I got up to speak, I talked about worship again and said that when we are truly worshipping, the heavens are opened and we are in touch with the Almighty. Then I told them about Vivian and the urologist, Major Gibbons, and there was huge applause – and then we continued our worship.

After the service, I baptized the four Iraqis in a private ceremony. They hadn't just been at the service the day before, they'd also come to the service in the Palace this evening. We had Communion together and once again the glory of God visited us.

Then it was time for the evening Alpha course, the 10-week introduction to basic Christianity we are running for Coalition staff. From the very beginning we worshipped and talked about God's glory in Iraq. People spoke of their pain and their joy, and how they had been called to this country. We finished at gone 10, and once again God's glory was there. Oh, how I praise God for this weekend in Iraq!

The next day we take Vivian to the military hospital, but she isn't allowed in as the right piece of paper hasn't been signed by the commanding officer. I go and see Major Gibbons with all her medical papers. He looks through them, and sees the CT scan. The tumour is large, and he thinks she may need to go to Washington DC. He promises to work on the case continually and I know he will. I go back to Vivian and her father and I tell them she may have to go to America. There is joy on her father's face that at last she is being treated.

I look again at her notes and see how serious her case is. I look at Vivian and I realize that I love this little girl as if she were my own. I think back to the days before the war, when I used to see so many children with terrible cancers, which were blamed on the depleted uranium in the weapons we have been using against Iraq since 1991. Vivian is one of these children. The tumour is huge and growing. God has worked wonderfully for her, but she is so ill. She and her family join us for dinner at our base, and after they leave I return to my political work. That night – my last in Baghdad for a little while – there are tears in my eyes as I pray for her.

The next morning, I leave early for the airport. I am wearing my body armour and surrounded by my wonderful guards. There is no safety briefing on this flight! In Kuwait, I am met from the plane as usual by Iraq's head of mission, Hamid al-Sharifi, a truly wonderful man. Once he worked with me and now he's in charge of Iraq's embassy to the country it once hated most. At night, he joins me for dinner with Frank Wismer, a great man who had been chaplain at the Palace in the days of the CPA and is now with the US Army in Kuwait. We are joined by the political-military officer [who liaises between the army and the embassy], who was also in Iraq during the war. The conversation is all about the growing conflict in Iraq, our love for that country and the need for more religious engagement to try to curb the sectarianism.

After dinner we retire to drink tea, and once again our conversation returns to Vivian. I phone Major Gibbons again and he is pleased to tell me that he has permission to see her the next morning. I fly back to England thinking about Vivian – and then go straight to meet the Archbishop of Canterbury and Mar Georges, the Archbishop of Baghdad in the Ancient Church of the East (New Calendar).

So, what is God doing in Iraq, and why all this glory? I will never forget the first time I saw it over Baghdad, or the countless miracles I have witnessed since then. I will never forget how my own experience has borne out the words of Ezekiel 43. I will also never forget a meeting I had in Jerusalem with an expert on Ezekiel at the Hebrew University who told me that God's glory never returned to Jerusalem after the exile in Babylon. It will return again, but only when the Messiah returns. And we are told that the glory will come from the East. What is east of Jerusalem? Iraq, the ancient Babylon. This is the place from which God's glory will return.

Few people have had the privilege to be here in Iraq; but many of those who have have seen God's glory. As the months have gone by, the glory has increased; but so has the violence. Here in our midst there is nothing less than a direct clash between the forces of God and his glory and the forces of Satan and his darkness. If there is any sign that the

Messiah will return soon, it is here. Here in the most dangerous place in the world, God is at work and his kingdom is coming. Those who come here and have the eyes of Christ see him. Here we see the power and the glory coming together. Here I am called to work not only in the political and diplomatic realms but also in the spiritual. Every meeting of God's people here is more glorious than the one before.

Two months later, Vivian had undergone major surgery and was out of hospital, playing with her brothers and her sister and looking wonderful. She has a very good chance of being cured and will remain in Jordan until her treatment is finished. All as a result of that weekend in August.

Clearly, my hope is more theological than political. We do not give up and one day, I know – though not soon – this place will be very different. The task ahead is huge, but so is the calibre of the Iraqi people. An immense encouragement to me has been the final verses of Isaiah 19, where we read that God has a special place not just for Israel but also for Egypt and Assyria – that is, Iraq.

In that day there will be a highway from Egypt to Assyria. The Assyrians will go to Egypt and the Egyptians to Assyria. The Egyptians and Assyrians will worship together. In that day Israel will be the third, along with Egypt and Assyria, a blessing on the earth. The LORD Almighty will bless them, saying, 'Blessed be Egypt my people, Assyria my handiwork, and Israel my inheritance.'

So, this is my hope, that Iraq will indeed one day be seen as the handiwork of God. This is my hope, still alight in the darkness, and I have no plan to give up on it.

Appendix 1

Accords

The Baghdad Religious Accord

24 February 2004

In the name of God who is Almighty, Merciful and Compassionate,

We who have gathered as clerics, intellectuals and political leaders representing all religions and doctrines pray and appeal for the peace of Iraq and declare our commitment to doing all in our power to ensure the ending of all acts of violence and bloodshed that deny the right to life, freedom and dignity. 'We have dignified humankind' [a verse from the Holy Qur'an].

According to our faith traditions, killing innocents in the name of God is a desecration of the laws of heaven and defames religion not only in Iraq but in the world.

We also declare to the world at large that:

1. The acts of corruption, violence and destruction are the work of the Devil that must be rejected by all as we seek together to rebuild our nation.

2. We, as Iraqis from different traditions, have decided to endeavour to live together as one family, respecting the moral and religious integrity of every individual, and we call upon all to condemn and renounce the culture of incitement, hatred and the defamation of the other.

3. The land of Iraq is holy in all scriptures. Therefore it is a duty for the followers of all divine religions to respect the sanctity of our land, whose good soil must not be desecrated by bloodshed.

4. The sanctity of all our places of worship and religious sites must be protected and preserved by all. The freedom of religious worship and expression must be guaranteed for all. 'No coercion in religion' [a verse from the Holy Qur'an].

5. We call on the political leaders in Iraq to work for a just, fair and peaceful transfer to democracy, inspired by the divinely inspired commandments of messengers and prophets.

6. We call on and urge the international community in the name of religion to assist us in the reconstruction of Iraq away from violence and chaos.

7. We shall endeavour to establish a process of truth, openness and reconciliation which will enable the spiritual, political, social and physical reconstruction of Iraq.

8. We shall devote ourselves to continue our joint efforts for the unity of the people of Iraq and for the creation of a climate of togetherness in which our present and future generations may live with mutual trust and respect. We shall also educate our present and future generations accordingly to maintain this commitment.

9. We, as clerics and intellectuals, ask those involved in politics and government not to slide down the slippery slope of sectarian politics, which has resulted in our present unstable situation; the absence of nationhood and the importation of alternative culture. Good governance should be based on citizenship and competence within a system of rights and obligations, irrespective of national, religious or racial affiliation.

10. We hereby announce the founding of the Iraqi Centre for Dialogue, Reconciliation and Peace (ICDRP), whose membership will be drawn from the people of Iraq and which will take a lead to ensure that the tenets of this accord are continuously implemented.

The Dokan Religious Accord

3 July 2004

In the name of God who is Almighty, Merciful and Compassionate,

We, clerics, intellectuals and social leaders representing all religions and doctrines in the Iraqi provinces of Nineva, Kirkuk, Arbil, Dhawk and Sulaymaniayah, who have gathered here at the Dokan resort in Sulaymaniayah, Iraq, pray and appeal for the peace of Iraq and declare our commitment to doing all in our power to ensure the ending of all acts of violence and bloodshed that deny the right to life, freedom and dignity. 'We have dignified humankind' [a verse from the Holy Qur'an].

According to our faith traditions, killing innocents in the name of God is a desecration of the laws of heaven and defames religion not only in Iraq but in the world.

We also declare to the world at large that:

1. The acts of corruption, violence and destruction must be rejected by all as we seek together to rebuild our nation.

2. We, as Iraqis from different traditions and societies, have decided to endeavour to live together as one family, respecting the moral and religious integrity of every individual, and we call upon all to condemn and renounce the culture of incitement, hatred and the defamation of the other.

3. The land of Iraq is holy in all scriptures. Therefore it is a duty for the followers of all divine religions to respect the sanctity of our land, whose good soil must not be desecrated by bloodshed.

4. The sanctity of all our places of worship and religious sites must be protected and preserved by all. The freedom of religious worship and expression must be guaranteed for all. 'No coercion in religion' [a verse from the Holy Qur'an].

5. We call on the political leaders in Iraq to work for a just, fair and peaceful transfer to democracy, inspired by the divinely inspired commandments of messengers and prophets.

6. We call on and urge the international community in the name of religion to assist us in the reconstruction of Iraq away from violence and chaos.

7. We shall endeavour to establish a process of truth, openness and reconciliation which will enable the spiritual, political, social and physical reconstruction of Iraq.

8. We shall devote ourselves to continue our joint efforts for the unity of the people of Iraq on the basis of fraternity and partnership and for the creation of a climate of togetherness in which our present and future generations may live with mutual trust and respect. We shall also educate our present and future generations accordingly to maintain this commitment.

9. We, as clerics and intellectuals, ask those involved in politics and government not to slide down the slippery slope of sectarian politics, which has resulted in our present unstable situation; the absence of nationhood and the importation of alternative culture. Good governance should be based on citizenship and competence within a system of rights and obligations, irrespective of national, religious or racial affiliation.

10. We hereby decide to establish our regional branch of the Iraqi Centre for Dialogue, Reconciliation and Peace (ICDRP), which will be based in the city of Kirkuk and whose membership will be drawn from the people of Iraq in the five provinces, who will take a lead to ensure that the tenets of this accord are continuously implemented.

Appendix 2

Who's who

al-Adin, Sayed Iyad Jamal
A leading Shia cleric who returned to Iraq in 2003 after many years in exile in Iran and the UAE.

al-Ani, Sheikh Abdel Karda
One of the key Sunni leaders of Iraq, with whom we worked in the early days after the war. He disappeared without trace after his house was bombed in May 2004 after he met with the CPA.

al-Badri, Sheikh Jamal
An important Sunni leader who was introduced to me by the American diplomat Andy Morrison. He has played a significant role in the new Ministry of Religious Affairs and helped to set up a coalition of Sunni leaders called Da'wa al-Fatwa.

al-Chaderchi, Nasir
A secular Sunni moderate who leads the National Democratic Party. A member of the Iraqi Governing Council.

al-Dari, Sheikh Dr Harith
A senior Sunni cleric who is the head of the Association of Muslim Scholars. I met with him on many occasions – the first time in the Mother of All Battles Mosque.

al-Duri, Izzat Ibrahim
Vice-chair of the Revolution Command Council and deputy commander-in-chief of Iraq's armed forces, and one of the ringleaders in the coup that brought the Ba'th Party to power in 1968.

al-Hakim, Ayatollah Muhammad Baqr
One of Iraq's best-known Shia leaders, who was killed by a huge car bomb in Najaf on 29 August 2003, he had just given a sermon on the need for Iraqi unity. His murderers were probably Sunni militants. He was head of the Supreme Council for the Islamic Revolution in Iraq (Sciri).

al-Hakim, Sayed Abdel Aziz

The leader of the United Iraqi Alliance and (after the murder of his brother, Ayatollah Mohammed Baqr al-Hakim, in August 2003) the Supreme Council for the Islamic Revolution in Iraq (Sciri). I met with him, bizarrely, in Tariq Aziz's old house. A member of the Iraqi Governing Council.

al-Khoi, Ayatollah Abdel Majid

A member of the Iraqi opposition from a very prestigious Shia family, who was assassinated in Najaf on 10 April 2003 – probably by followers of Muqtada al-Sadr. I had got to know him when he was living in exile in London.

al-Qabasi, Sheikh Ahmed

The most senior of Iraq's Sunna, still living in exile in Dubai, where he fled after falling out with Saddam, but exerting considerable influence in his own country through his televised sermons. I have met him several times.

al-Rubaie, Dr Mowaffak

A friend and disciple of Ayatollah Hussein al-Sadr who I first met in London in 1999. A member of the Iraqi Governing Council, who Paul Bremer subsequently appointed for five years as Iraq's National Security Adviser. While in exile, he had practised as a doctor in the London suburb of Ealing. He is the first chair of the Iraqi Institute of Peace.

al-Sadr, Ayatollah Hussein

My most important Shia ally in Iraq, and the 'father' of the Baghdad Religious Accord. I made his acquaintance on my first visit to Iraq. When he visited Britain in 1999, I learned that over 200 members of his family had been killed by Saddam's regime or had disappeared, but I discovered only later how cruelly he had been treated himself. He is a very holy man, and as moderate as his close relative, Muqtada al-Sadr, is extreme.

al-Sadr, Muqtada

The youngest son of Grand Ayatollah Mohammed Sadiq al-Sadr (who was assassinated in 1999 by agents of Saddam). After the war, he created a militia in Najaf known as the Mehdi Army. An Iraqi judge has issued a warrant for his arrest in connection with the murder of Ayatollah Abdel Majid al-Khoi, but he strongly denies the charge.

al-Tikriti, Qusay Saddam Hussein

Saddam's second son, and from 2000 his designated heir. He was believed to run the Mukhabarat and had some authority over the Republican Guard. He and his brother Uday were killed on 22 July 2003 in a shoot-out with 200 American troops backed by helicopters.

al-Tikriti, Uday Saddam Hussein

Saddam's eldest son, possibly a psychopath. He was head of Iraq's Olympics Committee and also commanded the Fedayin and controlled much of the Iraqi media.

al-Zarqawi, Abu Musab

The one-legged Jordanian who was the leader of the terrorist group al-Tawhid wa'al-Jihad ('Unity and Struggle'). He had close connections with al-Qa'ida and was widely believed to be behind much of the insurgency in Iraq. He was killed by an American air strike in June 2006.

al-Zubaydi, Professor Sadoon

My interpreter – and formerly Saddam's (and as such a familiar face from Iraqi television). He had previously been Iraq's ambassador to Indonesia and, before that, had taught Shakespeare in England.

Alfatlawi, Fadel

A member of our early team in Baghdad who eventually became the secretary general of the Iraqi Institute of Peace. I first met him in England, where he had fled as a teenager after the Ba'thists had killed his father and his brother.

Allawi, Dr Iyad

A secular Shia who co-founded the Iraqi National Accord party. A member of the Iraqi Governing Council, and then Prime Minister in the interim government. He joined the Ba'ath Party as a young man but fell out with Saddam in the early 1970s. While living in exile, he practised as a doctor in the London suburb of Wimbledon. He became the patron of the Iraqi Institute of Peace in June 2004.

Aziz, Tariq

Deputy Prime Minister of Iraq under Saddam and one of his longest-surviving comrades. Unusually for a senior figure in the regime, he is culturally a Christian and is not a member of the al-Tikriti clan. I met him many times, and notoriously took him some bottles of HP Sauce. I have not seen him since the war, though he gave himself up to the Coalition on 24 April 2003.

Bennetts, Colin
The Bishop of Coventry, under whom I have worked during most of my involvement with Iraq. He visited the country in 1999 and continues to play an active role in our work there.

Bidawid, Raphael I
The Chaldean Catholic Patriarch who visited America and Britain in 1999. He died in September 2003 and was succeeded by Immanuel III Deli.

Bremer, Paul
The American presidential envoy and administrator (or 'king') of Iraq from 6 May 2003 to 28 June 2004. He reported directly to the American Secretary of Defense, Donald Rumsfeld.

Chalabi, Ahmed
The secular Shia leader of the Iraqi National Congress, and a prominent member of the Iraqi Governing Council. For many years he was the Americans' favourite Iraqi – and the source of much of their 'intelligence' about Saddam's WMDs – but he fell from grace after the war and the Americans accused him of duping them as an agent of Iran.

Coalition Provisional Authority (CPA)
The international administration that ran Iraq from 6 May 2003 until the handover of sovereignty on 28 June 2004. It was completely dominated by the Americans, though the British played a significant role.

Cross, Major General Tim
One of three deputies to Lieutenant-General Jay Garner when he was running the short-lived Office of Reconstruction and Humanitarian Assistance in 2003. An expert on reconstruction, and a committed Christian.

Fedayin
A paramilitary organization numbering at most 40,000, whose name means literally 'Sacrificers'. It was not part of Iraq's armed forces but was totally dedicated to Saddam and put up a stiff and sometimes fanatical resistance to the Coalition advance.

Greenstock, Sir Jeremy

Britain's former ambassador to the UN, who served alongside Paul Bremer at the CPA as Britain's special representative in Iraq from September 2003 to April 2004.

Hammadi, Dr Abdel Majid

The director of Iraq's first-ever bone marrow transplant centre, at the Saddam Medical City in Baghdad.

Handford, Clive

The Bishop of Cyprus and the Gulf, who has oversight of both the Anglican Church in Iraq and me. In 1967 he was briefly the rector of St George's, Baghdad.

Hassan, Prince

The former Crown Prince of Jordan and the moderator of the World Conference on Religion and Peace. A strong supporter of our work, who told me that tolerance is not enough.

Humayem, Sheikh Dr Abdel Latif

The personal imam and close confidant of Saddam Hussein, who had made the pilgrimage to Mecca on his behalf and reportedly wrote a copy of the Qur'an in his blood. When he visited America and Britain in 1999, the CIA identified him as 'the Billy Graham of Baghdad'. After the war, he took refuge in Amman. We eventually secured his return to Iraq, but he fled back to Jordan in June 2004 after the National De-Ba'thification Committee seized all his assets.

International Centre for Reconciliation (ICR)

One of the world's oldest religious-based centres for reconciliation, established at Coventry Cathedral following the destruction of the medieval building in 1940.

Iraqi Centre for Dialogue, Reconciliation and Peace (ICDRP)

The original, unwieldy name of the Iraqi Institute of Peace.

Iraqi Governing Council (IGC)

The body of 25 prominent Iraqis established by the CPA in July 2003 to provide input into the running of their country until the handover of sovereignty to the interim government on 28 June 2004. Its members were all appointed by Paul Bremer, who had the power of veto over all its decisions.

Iraqi Institute of Peace (IIP)
The organization established by the Baghdad Religious Accord on 24 February 2004 to pursue peace and reconciliation in Iraq.

Iraqi Interim Government
The government that took power after the handover of sovereignty by the CPA on 28 June 2004. Its members, all Iraqis, were appointed by the UN special envoy Lakhdar Brahimi. It was to remain in power until the formation of a transitional government after the election of 30 January 2005.

Ja'fari, Dr Ibrahim
A devout Shia who is one of the key leaders of the Islamic Da'wa Party. A member of the Iraqi Governing Council and one of the two vice-presidents in the interim government. While living in exile in Britain, he practised as a doctor in the London suburb of Wimbledon.

Jones, Jerry
A close ally in the Pentagon, where he works in the Office of White House Liaison.

Kana, Yonadam
The secretary general of the Assyrian Democratic Movement and the only Christian member of the Iraqi Governing Council. He is a close ally and sits on the executive council of the Iraqi Institute of Peace.

Kicklighter, General Mick
A retired American three-star general who on behalf of the Pentagon co-ordinated Iraq's transition to sovereignty with Frank Ricciardone. He is a committed Christian.

Kingston, Tom
A project officer at the International Centre for Reconciliation, who managed its projects in Iraq.

Mandians
Adherents of a religion derived from the followers of John the Baptist.

Mohamed, Mrs Samia Aziz
The leader of the (Shia) Faili Kurds, who chairs the forum on women, religion and democracy at the Iraqi Institute of Peace and sits on its executive council.

Mubarak, Dr Umid

The Iraqi Minister of Health before the war was very different from the other members of Saddam's cabinet who I met. At his request, I arranged for training in England for the medical team at the Saddam Bone Marrow Transplant Centre in Baghdad. I met him many times, and we became friends. I have seen him since the war.

Mukhabarat

The Arabic word for 'intelligence', and hence the name of Saddam's intelligence service.

Raad, Prince

The rightful heir to the throne of Iraq and another strong supporter of our work.

Revolution Command Council

The committee of senior Ba'th Party members, chaired by Saddam Hussein, which effectually ruled Iraq.

Ricciardone, Frank

The American ambassador to the Philippines, who on behalf of the State Department co-ordinated Iraq's transition to sovereignty with the retired general Mick Kicklighter.

Richmond, David

Sir Jeremy Greenstock's deputy at the CPA, and then his successor as Britain's special representative in Iraq until the handover of sovereignty to the interim government on 28 June 2004.

Sada, Georges

A former air vice-marshal in the Iraqi airforce and president of the Protestant Churches of Iraq, who I met on my first visit to Baghdad in 1999. He became my right-hand man and the International Centre for Reconciliation's representative in Iraq, before being headhunted to run the new Ministry of Defence. He became chief spokesman for the new interim prime minister of Iraq, and then his special adviser.

Sawers, John

Britain's first special representative in Iraq. He was an old friend of mine who as ambassador to Egypt in 2002 had helped me to draft the Alexandria Declaration. He later became the political director of the Foreign Office.

Scutt, Oliver
A project officer at the International Centre for Reconciliation, who managed its projects in Israel/Palestine.

Segar, Christopher
The diplomat who looked after British affairs as head of the British Office Baghdad throughout the rule of the CPA. An invaluable friend and continuing supporter of our work

Sistani, Grand Ayatollah Ali
A man of great holiness and enormous influence, who (at least in his own country) refuses to meet anyone who is not Iraqi. He is moderate and I am told by Ayatollah Hussein al-Sadr and Dr Mowaffak al-Rubaie that he strongly supports our work – although he was not a great admirer of the new temporary constitution.

Smock, David
The director of initiatives on religion and peacemaking at the United States Institute of Peace. Another very close ally.

Symons, Baroness
The British Minister of State for the Middle East. She is a Christian and a great friend and supporter.

von Sponeck, Count Hans
Assistant Secretary-General of the UN, and its humanitarian co-ordinator for Iraq from October 1998 to February 2000, when he resigned in protest at the international policy towards Iraq, including sanctions. I first bumped into him in the foyer of al-Rashid in 1999, when he asked me if I played tennis.

Welby, Justin
Like me, a 'residentiary canon' of Coventry Cathedral and co-director of the International Centre for Reconciliation. His main interest is in Africa, and especially Nigeria.

Wismer, Frank
A colonel in the US Army who served as chaplain to the CPA.

Yazidi
Adherents of a religion with ancient origins in Zoroastrianism.